TALES IN THE INSULIN VIAL
Stories for Diabetics and Their Families

Steve Beriault

Raider Publishing International

New York　　　　London　　　　Johannesburg

ISBN: 1-61667-005-3
Published By Raider Publishing International
www.RaiderPublishing.com
New York London Johannesburg

Printed in the United States of America and the United Kingdom

THE BERIAULT FAMILY

Jean Paul & Lillian
Maria, Nick, Dan & Lindsay
Robert, Alex, Andrew
Mike & Sylvia
Karen, mother to John, Adam, Kaelin, Paul,
died June, 2002.
Anita
Marielle
Doris & Michelin
(Lillian & Jean Pierre Asselin)

FRIENDS

Roman Andruzko
Justin Bates
Robert & Hazel Bruce
John & Charlene DeLuca
Dr. Cliff & Grace Dobb
Frank & Teresa Dolinsek
Dr. Pat & Laurie Dooley
Drs. Don & Anne DuVall
Helen Faga
Dennis & Jane Higgison
Ray Hogeboom
Duane & Kathy MacDougall
May McKenzie
Mig Migirdycan
Keith, Paul, Pat, Tom Nephin
Diane & Colin Runnals
John & Ina Schellenberg
Janet Slaughter
Caroline & Robert Stanton

THANKS

UHN (Toronto General Hospital & Staff)
UHN (Toronto Western Hospital & Staff)
Toronto - St. Michael's Hospital & Staff
Toronto - Mount Sinai Hospital & Staff
Toronto - St. John's Rehabilitation Hospital & Staff
Richmond Hill - York Central Hospital & Staff (Dialysis)
Barrie - Royal Victoria Hospital & Staff
Newmarket – Southlake Hospital & Staff

CONTENTS

PREFACE

I was diagnosed with Type 1 diabetes (juvenile diabetes) in my second year and I decided to write these stories in my fifty-seventh year. Because I was diagnosed so young, I can't remember my first insulin injection— but I bet it hurt me. I know I must have cried. I am sure my parents wept as well to know their son would spend the rest of his life performing this life-saving ritual. I can't remember my first hypoglycemic episode either, but I know my parents were frightened when it happened. But despite all the things I can't remember in the beginning, I have lived a full life rich in loving memories of my family, friends and what I have accomplished despite my disease. I want to share those memories with you and hope they inspire you as they have others.

The ideas for the stories didn't occur all at once and I carried some in my mind for a long time. I finally put pen to paper and put all my thoughts in print in a little over a year. Some stories just happened unexpectedly while I was writing (i.e., "Diabetes Dies," "Don't You Just Love It When!," "Bully Boy" and "The Appointment") while others have been in my mind for years, like the stories about my kayak trip and my cross-Canada bike trip; and "Warriors," which talks about three eras of diabetes and the hope for the cure. In "Warriors," the first era refers to the time before insulin and the inescapable death sentence for young patients who developed diabetes in those days. Their slow deaths turned them into concentration camp skeletons ("We are the hollow men, we are the stick men") with no hope for survival. The second era is my generation, those who have lived with insulin and who have suffered and died from its use. It concerns the early days when the technology and spread of knowledge was lacking. My generation has taken the full brunt of the long-term complications of poor diabetes control. We have suffered the loss of limbs, eyesight, kidneys, nerve tissue and other end organs, leading to our untimely deaths. The third and future era is what all diabetics and their family's dream of, when a research savior will eliminate diabetes from the face of the earth. We all pray for this demon to be destroyed.

Some of the stories are fictional but have been written with a kernel of truth or personal experience buried inside them. For example, "The Appointment" relates the result of a bad medical appointment with an old army doctor who was just a little too much to bear; "Bully Boy" tells the tale of a big boy who thought he could push people around until he ran into a determined and fearless diabetic; "All in the Family" matches hockey triumph with the fearful night-time hypoglycemic reaction and how the family reacts; and "Opportunity Cost" describes how a small boy believes that going to diabetic camp will cause a magical event.

Other stories are non-fictional but all relate to diabetes and its effects. These include "Voyageur," the true story of the first diabetic (me) to bicycle across Canada from Vancouver to St. John's, Newfoundland; and "On the Rivers," about kayaking the old voyageur fur-trading route in Western Canada. The non-fictional stories also deal with kidney transplant and double amputation, and a failed attempt at a whole pancreas transplant to end the diabetic condition—all from a patient's perspective.

I haven't found another book like this in my review of diabetes literature. These tales take you from childhood through adolescence and into adulthood and show the challenges the diabetic condition presents and how those challenges were met. Many readers have told me they've found these stories informative and inspirational, and I hope you do too. Thank you for reading!

INTRODUCTION
The Boxer

The number of diabetics is growing aggressively and researchers have considered it pandemic. The worldwide diabetes population comprises almost 240 million persons. About 24 million of that total, or 10 percent, are Type 1 diabetics (insulin-dependent); while Type 2 diabetics (non-insulin-dependent) make up 216 million.

Sadly, I consider the growth of diabetes as our key to freedom. Our army of fighters is growing and can no longer be ignored. As our ranks fill and we struggle for life, we draw on more financial resources and depend on more skilled caregivers from our society to survive. In Canada, it is estimated that diabetes costs our health-care system $13 billion per year. Dialysis treatments alone cost $50,000 per year per person, and leg amputation costs $74,000 per diabetic. This cost will increase over time. A cure to end this waste in human beings and financial and human resources is required quickly.

We are not cured by insulin—that is the mythical story told by those who don't know or understand. We fight each day to monitor, regulate, diet and exercise in an attempt to achieve normal blood sugar control. The fight also includes education and funding research to find a cure. And still, each day that we fight, we cost society more to maintain our disease; yet we continue to lose more diabetics to kidney failure, blindness, leg amputations, heart problems and early death despite our heroic personal struggles. Our army of fighters must destroy diabetes once and for all!

THE BOXER

In the clearing stands a boxer
                    and a fighter by his trade
And he carries the reminders
                    of every blow that laid him low
Or cut him till he cried out
                    in his anger and his pain
I am leaving...
                    I am leaving...
But the fighter
                    still remains.

                                        Paul Simon

TALES IN THE INSULIN VIAL
Stories for Diabetics and Their Families

Steve Beriault

Tale #1
OPPORTUNITY COST

There isn't a day that passes that a diabetic child doesn't dream, deep in his or her heart, that he or she will never have to take insulin injections again. In reality, the child will do this for life or until a cure is found. In my young life, I had to have one injection every morning and I hated it. That later evolved into four injections a day in adulthood. Today, juvenile diabetics begin taking multiple injections—up to four or five per day—plus finger pricks for blood monitoring from the time they are diagnosed.

It was late. Through the small opening in the door to his room, the boy looked out upon the kitchen and watched his mom and dad talking. He should have been sleeping, but his mind was full of thoughts concerning things his mom had told him earlier in the day. She had told him about a wonderful opportunity to attend a camp for diabetics, like himself, where he could meet new friends, swim, canoe, hike, fish and play games. His mom seemed so excited and happy about telling him these things that he didn't share his real thoughts, like the fact that he could play games at home with his old friends—he didn't need new friends. He didn't understand what a camp or a canoe was, and he had seen a lake and it was too scary, big and dark to swim in. Anyway, he already swam at the pool in town, which was nice and clear and he could safely see the bottom.

The boy turned his head and pressed his ear towards the crack in the door and listened intently to hear what his parents were talking about. Mom was talking to Dad about the special camp. Dad was saying that the cost was too much for the family at the time. Mom replied that there was some sponsor (he couldn't make out the name) who was willing to pay the camp costs for some of the children. The doctor had recommended that the boy be sponsored. Dad voiced his surprise and commented gratefully on the generosity of some people. Both Mom and Dad seemed very happy about this. Dad said it would be a very worthwhile experience and would probably make the boy a new person. Mom said it would be a magical experience and he would be much better off for the time spent there.

He turned from the door and went back to his bed. What was this all about, this special camp where magical things happened that would change him? He assumed that whatever happened, it would be good for him because his mom and dad would not send him to a place where he might get hurt. Speaking of hurt, he remembered that he would have to take that hateful needle in the morning at camp, just like every morning. He had shed copious tears when he realized that he would have to take needles for the rest of his life. He was angry and resentful that such a thing had happened to him and he asked many times, "Why me?" He had done nothing to deserve this painful daily reminder that reinforced his anger and resentment at how life had been so unfair to him.

He lay angrily in the bed and thought about his situation. After some time it struck him: What if the magical and wondrous event that would make him a changed person meant … could it possibly be … that he'd never have to take needles again? Was that what was so special about this camp and why mom and dad were so happy about his chance to go there?

He trembled with excitement at the thought of that delicious freedom. He would not have to take any needles anymore. He would be free! It couldn't be simpler. The answer was as clear as the nose on your face. His mom and dad couldn't say anything because that would ruin the magic. It would be like being surprised at Christmas when Santa brought you a special gift. He would have to keep quiet and pretend he didn't know anything. It was their special secret for the special camp.

He was very happy over the following weeks waiting for the day that he would travel on the bus to the camp. Time seemed to fly by and all the while he kept the magical secret to himself. He wondered if any other kids knew what was going to happen, if any of them had figured it out and if they might spoil it for everyone if they told somebody accidentally. He couldn't wait to go.

Finally, the big day arrived, and early in the morning he was the first down to the beat-up, rusted old yellow Volkswagen van. Dad was proud of his VW van, as it had taken him everywhere during his college days and he had dated his mom in the "van." However, it was so beat up that he had to coax it into second gear because the transmission was going on it. After these gear shifts, Dad would say to the van, "Way to go sweetheart," in encouragement.

The family had to drive to the meeting place where he would board the bus with the rest of the kids. Both the boy's mom and dad commented how pleased they were about his apparent enthusiasm for the camping experience. How could he not be, given what he'd figured out!

Soon they arrived at a large church parking lot, where three yellow school buses stood. There must have been about one hundred kids standing around waiting. The boy was amazed at the number of kids with diabetes, all of different sizes and ages. In his mind, he had assumed there were only a few unlucky ones like him, but this parking lot full of kids sure proved he was wrong. He certainly was not alone taking those painful and hateful needles. But soon, he knew, that would end for all of them. He wondered how many of these kids had also figured out the secret of the camp. Hopeful, he looked around to see if anyone appeared to be hiding something. No such luck! There wasn't even a hint from anyone.

Soon he kissed, hugged and said goodbye to his parents and climbed onto the bus. He had heard that the trip would be long, about one hundred miles, and that there would be a break at the halfway point for snacks and bathroom. He enjoyed the trip and found that some of the kids were so full of energy they wouldn't sit down for two seconds. They were running, singing, yelling and throwing things around the bus. The counselors had to come back several times to settle everybody down. Most of it was really fun, but the ride seemed very long.

As the bus passed through the camp gates, the boy began to tremble with excitement. He wondered if there would be some kind of unique moment or feeling when the magic happened. He thought it probably would happen in the nighttime when they were sleeping; magic worked best at night. He envisioned an announcement as they went for their morning injections at the infirmary:

SPECIAL ANOUNCEMENT
Boys and Girls,
Thank you for attending our
SPECIAL DIABETIC CAMP

Over the nighttime, an extraordinary magic spell has entered your body, created by the world's greatest magical researcher, to end the need to take needles. You will no longer be required to come to the INFIRMARY for needles ever again. Please enjoy your camping experience.

— THE CAMP MANAGEMENT

He quickly snapped out of his daydream as the bus came to a halt and the counselors asked the kids to carefully get out of the bus. Of course several kids did not follow the instructions and they fell over each other trying to get out of the bus first. The counselors just shook their heads and lifted them up.

The camp was cut out of the bush, and the dark-green pine trees were like sentinels encircling the main area. The kids were directed to a big building called the Great Hall made of logs and wood. Along the walls were Indian art pieces and special camping awards given to campers over the years. A large canoe hung from the ceiling. The dining area was a huge room with two large stone fireplaces and tables and chairs set for supper. Each place setting had a child's name on a slip of paper, so that everyone would know where to sit. The chatter around the table was exciting and funny. Soon everyone was settled and they were all wondering what was next.

In stepped a huge man dressed in tawny leather garb with beads and a huge Indian eagle-feather war bonnet. He was very impressive and stood silently until not a sound was heard in the large room. He introduced himself in a loud powerful voice as Chief Wandering Horse, the camp director. He then went on to welcome the children to the camp and individually introduced the camp counselors, who were seated with the children at the tables.

The counselor at the boy's table was called Single Feather (but they would soon learn his real name was Jim) and he was an older person with a white beard, graying hair and blue eyes that seemed to be constantly watching and monitoring. He didn't miss much. He was first up to help one of the kids at their table who'd slipped into insulin reaction. The kid was white in the face; he was sweating and his hands were shaking. Most kids didn't even know what was going on, but Single Feather did. Quickly and quietly, he got the kid a box of apple juice and sat with him till supper was served.

Chief Wandering Horse informed the campers that the name mounted in the center of their table was the name of their tent, and that would be their home for the time they were at camp. The boy's tent was called the "Tamarack." The youngest members at the camp were in that tent and

5

the tent beside them, called the "Blue Spruce." The tents held nine kids per tent and one counselor. Chief Wandering Horse then said he would make more announcements the next day, but now he wanted them all to have supper, get their bags and go and see their tents and get to know their counselors. He said the counselors knew all about the camp and would answer any questions the kids might have. He mentioned that many of the counselors were original campers and therefore diabetics as well.

The Tamarack and Blue Spruce kids were the first to leave the Great Hall. They were so excited they were tripping over themselves in their haste to get outside where their bags were. The boy grabbed his bag and waited for the others. Some needed help because their parents had packed too much stuff, but soon everyone was following Single Feather down the trail to the tents. As they walked along, Single Feather pointed out a white building.

"That's where the infirmary is," he announced. "You'll all go there in the morning."

The boy thought to himself, Bet that's when we find out.

It wasn't far and soon they were at Tamarack. Their names were on their cots, but Single Feather said if they wanted to change places, for whatever reason, they could discuss it with the other person and see if they wanted to change their cot location. The boy liked his location, which was in the center of the tent directly behind Single Feather's cot, and was not interested in going anywhere else. All the kids settled in quickly, storing their stuff under the beds and unrolling their sleeping bags. Single Feather pointed out the wash house and washroom, which were only a short distance away. He said, "Keep your flashlights handy, in case you have to go to the washroom at night. If you need help, just wake me."

As the sun went down, the kids began to chat and get to know each other. Some had brought checker and chess sets and were playing with newfound friends. Others were reading Batman and Superman comics or books on their cots. At different times, as questions came up, they would ask Single Feather for instruction and information. It was all very relaxed and friendly. The boy lay upon his cot and listened and didn't say much. His thoughts wandered to what would happen the next day and how excited everyone would be when they found out what he had figured out already. With those pleasant thoughts in mind, he drifted off to sleep.

The next morning, he heard a persistent and loud clanging sound somewhere in his head and opened his eyes to a sunny day. Single Feather was getting everyone up, saying the wake-up bell was ringing. They had passed a huge shiny bronze metal bell outside the Great Hall last night and this was used to signal campers about events over the course of the day. Quickly, everyone was up and listened to Single Feather's instructions concerning the morning wash-up and brushing of teeth. Then they all charged out of the tent and went over to the wash house to get prepared for the day.

Single Feather waited until everyone was done and had returned to the tent. Then he asked if everyone remembered where the infirmary was. Everyone chorused, "Yes."

"Well," he said, "let's see who can run there the fastest!" And the kids took off, running as fast as they could to see who would get to the infirmary first.

However, the boy held back and followed at the end of the pack. He wanted to see how the kids would react as they arrived at the infirmary. What would they do? How would they respond to this unexpected surprise? As the infirmary came into sight, he could see the first kids get to the door and they bolted inside. He delayed a little more and watched to see if anything might happen. More kids reached the infirmary door and went in. Still there was nothing. Finally, all the kids except him were in the infirmary. He waited at the corner of the building. Why didn't he hear screams and shouts of joy or see kids running out of the infirmary in a high state of excitement?

He slowly edged towards the infirmary door. Maybe everyone was in such shock and disbelief that they couldn't believe what was happening? Finally at the edge of the door he peeked in. The kids were circling around, talking to the nurses and either testing their urine or taking their own needles, and some nurses were helping others take their needles. He felt his heart sag and for a second he couldn't catch his breath. It was all false! It was all a lie! He would have to take those lousy needles forever. His shock soon turned to rage and he yelled at the top of his lungs, "NO!"

Everyone in the infirmary was startled and turned to look at him in surprise. He began to run. He was getting out of this place as fast as he could go. He was never coming back to this stupid camp. He was going to hide in the forest and they would never find him again!

He ran as fast and as hard as he could across the parking lot, past the Great Hall and the huge bronze bell and onto the gravel road, which the buses had used to get him to camp. He ran down the gravel road and towards the forest.

Finally, he saw the road bending to the left, and to the right he saw a path leading into the forest. He charged down the path at a very fast clip. The path was cut through old-growth pine and spruce, and the branches swiped his face and stung him. He began to cry in his frustration and anger, and soon his tears were so great that he sometimes lost sight of the path. At one of those moments, running totally blind, he was suddenly stopped.

In the distance, he heard a dim sound like "thunk." He was paralyzed, and for a second he was standing and then, in slow motion, he was falling. He fell on his back into thick weeds and grass that grew along the path, and strangely he enjoyed the coolness of the plant bed on his back and neck. Then he began to see lights blinking like stars in his field of vision, but he couldn't see anything else.

Everything in his mind was moving slowly and he felt deliciously tired. He felt he would enjoy staying in this state for a long time. Then from a long distance away he could hear a voice, though he couldn't make out what the voice was saying. But he really didn't care what the voice was saying and he wanted to ignore it but it wouldn't go away. Finally, he decided he would focus on the voice and see why it was so persistent.

He slowly opened his eyes and tried to focus on the face in front of him. "Hey buddy," the voice said, "welcome back to the land of the living." The boy groaned and noticed his head was hurting badly. He began to focus and understand things around him and finally he recognized Single Feather's face and voice.

"What happened?" he said, weakly.

"Well, you bumped your head," Single Feather said, and told him to lie quiet and rest for a little while. Single Feather gently massaged his face, neck and head with his hands and it relieved some of the aching that he felt in his head. After a while Single Feather said, "Are you feeling any better?"

"Yes," he answered.

"Do you want to try and sit up?"

"Yes," he said again, so Single Feather helped him sit up.

As he looked around he noticed he was sitting by the side of the path in long grass. The trees had fallen away to reveal a pond located to his right, thick with bulrushes and yellow flowering plants. Overhead, many birds were flying around. He turned his aching head slightly and gazed up at a huge old maple tree standing before him.

The path he'd been running on had split in two and continued left and right around the tree. He grabbed his head and couldn't believe what he had just done: he had run smack into a tree! The counselor snorted as he saw that the boy had figured out what had happened. Single Feather said that it was the classic case of the unstoppable force meeting the immovable object, and he laughed. He pulled out his radio communicator and informed the infirmary he had the boy and was bringing him back shortly. They sat for a while in silence.

Finally the boy felt strong enough to try to stand up and Single Feather helped him get to his feet. As they walked back down the path, Single Feather kept a hand on his shoulder in case he got weak or dizzy again, but he felt much better now except for his sore head. They walked in silence until they came back to the main gravel road. Finally the boy said, "You must think I'm a fool running through the forest like an idiot."

The counselor did not answer immediately and just kept walking. The silence seemed like forever but finally Single Feather spoke. "I've been at this camp for a long time and I've seen many things. Running away seems to be one of many different behaviors that young campers' exhibit when they're upset. They behave inappropriately because they miss their parents, or are having personal problems with another camper, or are afraid of swimming or canoeing in the lake, or are afraid to go on hikes in the forest because they think wild animals will attack them. There are many reasons that kids in a new, unfamiliar place might get scared, panic and do things you wouldn't expect. Thank God we've always been able to address the issues and managed to overcome their fears by talking to them."

As they walked on, the boy thought about Single Feather's words. Then he said, "I ran because I didn't want to take any more needles." Single Feather looked at him and said that a long time ago there was another young lad who had run away for the very same reason.

"He ran up the same trail you were on but he didn't run into the tree. Instead, he took the right fork, which is a very long trail, along the lake. The trail leads back to the camp and comes out right behind our tent at Tamarack. He hid there most of the day while we searched for him. Finally, I spotted him sleeping in some bushes right by the tent. He was not happy and was very hungry."

He waited but Single Feather didn't say any more. The boy said, "So what happened to him?"

Single Feather said that he went on to have a great

camp experience, and later he returned to the camp to become a counselor for several years. In fact, Single Feather said that the young man went on to bicycle five thousand miles across Canada—the first diabetic to do that. The boy remembered the huge wall map of Canada in his classroom. He knew Canada was very big but he could not understand what five thousand miles was like. It sounded like a huge and impressive number. So he said, "How long is five thousand miles?"

Single Feather replied, "It's very long." Then the counselor said, "Do you remember when we got on the bus to come to the camp, we told you the trip would be about one hundred miles and it took us almost all day to get there? Well you would have to take that trip fifty times, day after day, on a bicycle, through rain, heat and cold, strong winds, up mountains and down, and across wide prairies. You would carry all your supplies on your bike, like a tent, sleeping bag, food, water, insulin and needles." Single Feather looked at him and said, "Not bad for a young fellow who ran away because he didn't like needles."

The boy nodded in deep thought.

They continued to walk at a slow, leisurely pace. His sore head was getting better and he realized he was really hungry. He thought for a while in silence about what had happened on the path, and he also thought about what he and that other boy had in common. Then he saw the infirmary come into view and he turned to Single Feather, grinned and said, "You know, I have a bicycle at home."

Diabetic Camp 1957- The Old Brewery Mission
(Steve, standing near top of stairs, striped shirt,
scratching his head)

Tale # 2
BULLY BOY

As a young diabetic growing up in a working-class
neighborhood I was picked on for being different. I tried to
keep my secret well hidden, but having insulin reactions in
the middle of class-time was a dead giveaway that I was
not "the same."

     I was in grade school and I had kept my secret
pretty well hidden from the rest of the class. The only
person who knew I was diabetic was my teacher. My mom
and I had come for a meeting before classes started to make
sure Mrs. Gaul understood about diabetes in general and
more specifically about diabetic reaction. Since Mrs. Gaul
had diabetes in her family, she was very familiar with the
condition and the effects of low blood sugar
(hypoglycemia). My mom felt much better about my going
to school knowing that someone understood how diabetes
might unexpectedly affect my behavior and physical state.
     Although I met a lot of nice friends in my class,
none of them had a real interest in sports like I did,
especially football. During the day at school, with limited
resources, we would play mostly dodge ball on a marked,
paved section or run around playing tag on the grass
section. However, in the evening, after school, I would
always be at the park trying to get kids my age to play
sports like soccer, baseball, or football. They seemed to
have a low level of interest in any organized activity; they
would only play for a while and then wander off to do other
things.

13

I used to watch the older boys, about twelve years old, play football every evening until the sun went down at the far end of the park. That's what I wanted to do and I tried several times to join them, but they said their teams were already balanced and that I was too small to play with them. Luckily, my dad would come out several evenings during the week to throw the football to me and some of the kids who wanted to participate. On the weekends, I would religiously watch our black and white TV, which my dad got secondhand and repaired, for the football games.

At first when playing with my dad I had trouble catching the ball, but we continued practicing. My dad then pulled me aside and said, "You know your baby brother at home?" I nodded yes. "You know he is very precious to us?" I nodded and said I loved him. "He's just a little bigger than this football." Again, I agreed. Dad said, "What would happen if any of us dropped him?"

I immediately responded, "I would never drop him."

He said, "I know you wouldn't do that, son. Now think of the football as a precious thing and say, 'I will never drop the football when I try to catch it.' "

I remembered that and took it to my heart as my credo.

Meanwhile, back at school, a new kid was introduced to our class. He was big for his age. We learned his name was Joe; however, he liked to be called "Big Joe." We soon found out he had a propensity for picking on kids—both verbally and physically—who were smaller than he was. He managed to attract an assortment of bad apples and troublemakers who became his personal sycophants. Within a week of his arrival, he and his pals were stealing lunches that were better than theirs and pushing people into their lockers and locking the door on them. Joe and his buddies were never punished for these actions because the kids were so scared that they wouldn't tell the teachers who did it.

Maybe it was because Mrs. Gaul was checking on

me every so often or maybe it was just luck, but Big Joe and his gang of losers never approached me during the first month of their reign of terror. However, little did I know that this situation would soon change dramatically after an incident related to my diabetes.

A short while before that incident, though, I was at the park one evening by lucky chance when one of the older boys came over to me and asked if I was still interested in playing football. I caught my breath and said, "Do you mean me?" as I pointed to myself.

"Yeah," he laughed, "I mean you."

I found out that one of their friends had moved out of town and they were short a player to make a balanced game. Since they couldn't find anyone else, they selected me to play with them. I was so excited my heart was going crazy in my chest and I found myself getting short of breath. The game began and the quarterback (QB) said to me, "Just take it easy and don't do anything crazy. These guys are bigger than you and you could get hurt."

Getting hurt was the last thing on my mind. I wanted to get my hands on the ball. Thanks to my dad, I had developed the sense that when I was catching and carrying the football, I was holding something precious and I couldn't drop it or allow anyone to take it. I had to get to safety— the end zone—in any way possible when the ball was wrapped in my arms. But sadly, my first game was a big disappointment.

Although I helped on tackles and defensive plays, which I got congratulations for by some of the older fellows, on offense, I was not given one look by our QB. So even though I was open many times for passes, I was basically ignored. I was upset but I didn't say anything. I figured I was lucky enough to play this time and that I'd better let well enough alone.

Next day after school, I was at the park as fast as I could get there. I was the first kid there and I sat on the grass and waited. Soon I saw the QB arrive and he had his football with him.

fine. Then, quite unexpectedly, Big Joe came by and said, "I hope you're feeling better," and reached to shake my hand. Hmm, I thought, that's quite nice of him. However, when he grasped my hand he tried to crush it in his grasp and wouldn't let go. He then leaned close and said, "We are going to have fun with you, sweetie."

Although I was smaller, I wasn't afraid of him like the others in my class were. So I didn't let on his grasp on my hand was hurting, and I stared him in the face and smiled. He didn't like that, but just then Mrs. Gaul entered the classroom and asked everyone to be seated.

I knew I was in trouble and I saw no way out of it. This gorilla and his cronies were planning to make my life hell for as long as it pleased them or until they could find someone else to pick on. It started that afternoon when I went to my locker and found the door bent and out of shape. It looked like someone had kicked it in. I spoke to the maintenance man about it and he remarked that that was the sixth locker door destroyed like that in the past month.

A short time later, I was surrounded by Big Joe and his gang and he asked me if I always fell down when I went "weird." Before I could answer, he pushed me and I fell backwards over one of his buddies, who had positioned himself behind my legs. I landed heavily on the ground and they all crowded around me and used their feet to keep me down. Big Joe gave me an extra kick but I didn't cry or react fearfully. I just folded my arms over my chest, lay prone and waited silently until they got tired of standing over me. They finally left.

The next event occurred a few days later at noon; my lunch was stolen from the shelf in the back of the room. I knew who had taken it but I pretended I didn't know. So I went up and down the tables asking people if they'd seen my lunch anywhere. Soon, I arrived at my target group. I could see that one of Big Joe's punks was eating from my lunch bag, but I pretended not to notice.

"Hi, Big Joe," I said in my brightest voice and smiled and looked directly into his face. He ignored me. I said, "I just wanted to warn you that my lunch has been stolen."

Big Joe stopped eating for a second and then looked at me with a smirk. "Warning me about what?" he said in a grumpy voice.

"That my lunch has been stolen."

"Why do I have to be warned about your stupid lunch?"

Then he and his cronies started laughing. I waited and finally they stopped, because they wanted to hear what I was going to say. I paused before speaking—a long pregnant pause—as they hung on for my next statement.

"Well," I said slowly, "if you see anyone eating my lunch, could you tell them that I'm on a lot of medications for my condition? If you remember, the other day I had a reaction to one of the hormones that I take to help me, and a lot of those medications are included in the food I eat." Of course I was lying.

Big Joe hesitated because he didn't understand what a hormone was. He was now on unfamiliar ground. Then he said, "Well, what would those medications do to someone who might eat your lunch?"

"Well," I said, slowly again, "they wouldn't hurt me because I've been taking them for years. But for a person who's never had these drugs before, it could cause all kinds of bad things to happen."

I waited.

Suddenly the twit who was eating my lunch said, in a scared voice, "Yeah? What could happen?"

"Well," I replied, crisply and confidently, "Diarrhea, vomiting, seizures, pains in the chest, cramps, bloating and unstoppable flatulence." I stared at Big Joe right in the face, and he turned bright red. His buddy spat my sandwich out of his mouth and gulped some water to try to clean his mouth. So, I went on, "Please warn anybody you see eating my lunch that they should go to the doctor immediately. See you!"

I then went to the infirmary to get my back-up lunch

prepared by my mother for just such a case. Sure enough, the twit was missing from class that afternoon.

The next day, Big Joe came over to me and I smiled at him but he didn't smile back. He said, "My buddy went to the doctor yesterday and there was nothing wrong with him."

I looked at him and said, "Yes, I know. My mom forgot to put my drugs in my sandwich yesterday and so it was a false alarm." Then I said, "Aren't you and your friends glad?"

He said in a furious voice, "You're going to pay for that!"

Staring him in the face and smiling, I answered, "Well, I hope it's not too expensive." With that he stormed to the back of the class, where his seat was, and conferred with his spiritually destitute band of cowards and "no minds."

So, the pressure seemed to be off for the next couple of days as Big Joe and his gang remained quiet and out of sight. Once, on my way home, I thought I saw one of the gang but I couldn't be sure. In any case, I played football with the guys that night and had a great time. The QB was coming early now to throw long balls to me as extra practice. I loved the comments and corrections he offered. I learned that his dad was a university football coach and that he wanted to be a professional football player when he got older. I wondered if I could do that also.

The next day at school, I found my suspicions had been correct. I had been followed by one of Big Joe's thugs. Big Joe sauntered over to my desk and said, "My boys have been thinking of taking on the class in a football game. Do you think you're man enough to take us on?"

Be still my crazily beating heart! Did he just say what I thought he said? Oh my God!

"Great idea," I answered sweetly, "as long as you guys don't try to hurt anybody."

"Us?" he said. "We wouldn't even think of hurting anybody in particular." And he looked balefully into my eyes.

I was so excited I could barely sit still. Would I? Would I! I couldn't wait to take this gorilla on. Although he was much stronger than I was, he had no speed; he was awkward and clumsy, and he had greatly underestimated my spirit and desire to win. His cronies were no better than he as they weren't especially fast, intimidating or big, and had never played football before.

The fight would be essentially between me and Big Joe. The rest of the kids would be pylons in the game. Most of my team really didn't want to play but they were afraid of angering Big Joe, so they resigned themselves to at least standing on the field. The few who wanted to do it could not tackle Big Joe even if they wanted to; he would overpower them.

So, I came to a strategic decision. No one would even try to tackle Big Joe. We'd just let him run every time he got the ball. However, our team had to run after him as if we were going to tackle him. I figured the longer we made Big Joe run fast, the quicker he would tire out. Meanwhile, for every touchdown Big Joe got, I would match it. Big Joe and the rest of his pack were not fast enough to catch me. We, therefore, would wait patiently for mistakes and opportunities to happen throughout the game to gain our victory

Game day was a beautiful warm and sunny fall day. It was an absolutely perfect time for a football game. I felt so wonderfully alive and ready to play the game of my life. The opponents were lined up at the far end of the field, where the maintenance man had put markings on the grass for us. In their arrogance, Big Joe's team skipped the coin toss and volunteered to kick first to us.

The thinking was simple: Big Joe was going to try and kick the ball directly to me and then punish me for catching it. I couldn't wait. The ball was well kicked. Big Joe had a powerful leg, and I caught it deep in our zone and sprinted down the field. It was too easy. A quick head fake to the right, a stutter step, and I flew by Joe and his crew like they were standing still. I loved the look of incredulity on Joe's face as I turned on the speed and left him in my dirt.

So then we kicked to our opponents and we tried to keep it away from Joe, but his mate caught the ball and handed the ball off to Joe. He lumbered down the field, daring the kids to try and tackle him. Sure enough, the guys on my team chased him as we had discussed, and by the time he crossed the goal line, I could hear him breathing heavily. He wouldn't last long.

They kicked again: another beauty, very long but aimed away from me this time. My guys fumbled around with the ball but finally got it under control. As I looped back into our end zone, Big Joe's team smelled blood; they roared down on my fellow player and forgot about me. Suddenly, I appeared behind my teammate and he turned and handed the pigskin to me. The other team was so focused on my teammate that they were caught completely by surprise and I ran to the end zone again.

This is how the battle continued through the lunch period. We were running Big Joe ragged and he was sweating badly. On his fourth touchdown, I ran parallel to him but just out of reach, all the way down the field. It drove him crazy as he was lusting for some physical resolution. On the next touchdown by Big Joe, I ran ahead of him by a slight margin and he almost had a hernia trying to catch me so he could physically punish me.

When he got to the end zone, he knelt down for a long while to catch his breath. It didn't matter what their team did, the score was always in our favor and they were always catching up. In the second half, however, the roles were reversed. We had to kick first and Big Joe and team were in the advantage position in scoring. But Joe was getting greatly fatigued. He gave up chasing me on my last touchdown run.

It was late in the game when we kicked to Joe's team again. We aimed the kick to the left side of the field, where their weakest man was located. Sure enough, he fumbled the ball and tried desperately to get it under control. Big Joe was waiting for his pal to hand it off to him but the boy was clumsy and too slow and our team was on him. He fell on the ball so that he didn't lose it. This, then, was actually the first offensive play from scrimmage in our game. Joe called his huddle. I guessed there were three things that would happen. Joe would have the ball snapped to him and he would run with it (but I sensed he was getting really tired), or he could try to throw it to his best underling, or his best underling would throw it to him.

The opposition's huddle broke, and tired Joe decided to try and throw the ball. I told our defensive rushers to just pressure Joe but not try to tackle him. I didn't want anyone to get hurt. The play developed and Big Joe went back to pass. He drilled a really hard pass to an open man, but the boy could not catch it. It had too much speed on it.

As I looked up, I saw one of my guys on the ground. I raced over to see what the problem was. It seemed that when Joe's pass was not caught by his receiver, the big fellow reacted angrily by kicking at the closest person to him, saying, "Stay away from me, you little runt." He had gone too far and I stared at him for a good minute trying to control myself. He was daring me to do something because he wanted to give me a beating.

I didn't respond to his dare except to yell to him, "You're one hell of a lousy passer!" He got flustered by that and went back to his huddle. I hoped he would take the bait. It was almost too predictable. Of course, Big Joe was not going to accept that he was a lousy passer.

His team lined up in a passing formation and I knew who was going to receive the ball. The right halfback was wiping the sweat of his hands again, just as he had in the last pass attempt. I waited in the defensive backfield and watched the right halfback. He acted like he wasn't going to get the ball. He was slow off the line but he cut quickly to the inside looking for the pass. Joe reared back and this time softly laid the pass to his open teammate. That made it all the more easy for me to intercept.

I broke to the outside with the ball but this time I had no interest in getting a touchdown. I was looking for Big Joe. I ran directly towards him. He was going to pay for hurting that kid and for the other things he had done. I saw a smile on Joe's face as he realized what was finally going to happen: the physical battle he had been waiting for. But what he didn't realize was that I was going to be a human torpedo hitting the big battleship.

I increased my speed and fearlessly drove directly at him head first. At the last second, Big Joe realized what was happening and said, "What the hell are you doing?"

Too late! I drove myself into his chest and I could hear a crack and the wind whooshing out of his mouth. He landed on his back with a thunk! Somehow, although dizzy, I was still on my feet and I handed the ball to one of my guys and said, "Get us a touchdown."

We didn't see Big Joe for almost a month. We heard that he had three broken ribs. Mrs. Gaul was very upset with the game of football. She said it was a very savage sport and she would not allow it at the school again. The maintenance man became a good friend of mine and said with a smile, "Some people deserve a good 'wuppin' on the sports field," but he didn't mention any names.

Joe came back a changed person. He acted politely and helped people and was always the guy to help break up fights among the kids. He later became a good friend of mine and I went to his first university varsity football game, where he played right defensive linebacker. Oh! I was the offensive halfback on the opposing team. I looked straight into his eyes from my position all game long.

Tale # 3
THE APPOINTMENT

As a young boy I had many hospital visits to check my condition. All my diabetic friends used to speak about their doctors and whether they got along with them. There seemed to be one recurring theme: that old army doctors from the war were demanding and intolerant, and none of the kids liked them.

I absolutely hated the hospital appointments required every three months to get a check on my diabetic condition. I didn't want to go because I usually got stabbed with this big needle so blood could be drawn from my arm to check my blood sugar. The nurses would always smile and say, "It won't take a second," or "It won't hurt," or "You are such a big boy." I wanted to say, "YES, IT HURTS AND STOP SMILING ABOUT IT!"

I was in grade school and, as usual, Mom told me the night before that I would miss a day of school because we were going to see the doctor. She never said we were going to the hospital to get another needle, although we both knew what was going to happen. I wondered if anyone ever counted up how many needles a diabetic had to take over his or her lifetime. Not just the insulin injections, but all the blood tests and other things we got a needle for when we went to the hospital. The hospital, doctors and needles were the plague in every diabetic's life as far as I was concerned. Why couldn't they just leave us alone?

The only thing I liked going to the hospital for was the nice lady doctor who took care of me. I didn't like her in the beginning, but she asked all kinds of neat questions about me: what sports I liked, what interested me at school, what foods I liked to eat, if I was ticklish, if got along with my brothers, if I loved my mom and dad.

She didn't bring up anything about diabetes at that first meeting. She measured me, took my weight and checked my blood pressure, pulse, heart, eyes and feet, and that was pretty much all—no boring discussion about insulin, diet and taking care of myself. She talked to me and made me giggle and tickled me and then she said, "You can go down to the play yard and let me talk to your mother for a little while."

The play yard at the hospital was a grand place. It had every type of swing and monkey bar, ropes to climb, tunnels to climb into, and slides of all sizes. Also available were tennis balls, miniature basketballs with nets, miniature footballs, little hockey sticks and plastic hockey pucks, and a huge play area so you could play all by yourself or play as a group. I grabbed a miniature hockey stick and puck and went over to the hockey net to shoot the puck. Soon my mother came and we left the hospital, climbed into the bus and went back home.

On the way, Mom said, "What did you think of that doctor?"

I said she was nice.

"So would you like to go back to see her again?"

I hesitated and said, "No, not really," thinking that this was an invitation to go to the hospital more often than the every three months I was already going.

My mom understood immediately and said we would still only go to the hospital every three months, but that woman would be the doctor we would see when we went. (I wanted to negotiate and say that, if we could go only every twelve months, she would be the doctor I saw.) I said that would be okay. So this was how I got this lady doctor who made it fun to visit with her. But I still had to take the blood sugar needles. I asked her when they would stop and she commented that she was not a miracle worker.

As we drove along on the bus on appointment day, Mom said, "You'll be seeing a different doctor today because your regular doctor has gone to a conference in the United States."

Darn! I didn't like the idea of seeing a new doctor; I didn't know who it would be. What if it was one of those old army doctors who had come home from the war? They would order you around and tell you what you had to do, no questions asked. I was not looking forward to this visit at all.

Furthermore, Mom and Dad were having a hard time although they never said anything to me about it. I heard them talking late at night when I couldn't sleep. I stole out of my room, went down the hall to the kitchen, hid in a nook and listened. Dad's union had gone on strike and he wasn't making money now. My mother was saying that they had some savings and that she could take care of some of the neighbor's kids to make extra money. My father said he had to take his shift on the picket line but when he finished that responsibility, he could take a part-time job in the evenings. They both sounded really worried.

I could see my mom was distracted and worried as she sat on the bus with me. She was unusually quiet and wasn't pointing things out to me as she normally did when we rode on the bus. I tried to make her laugh by making silly faces and she smiled and hugged me. But her demeanor did not change much.

We arrived late for our appointment because it was pouring rain and the bus had to slow down. Also, a lot of last-minute passengers had run for the bus, trying to get out of the rain. So the bus driver had waited for these people. The appointment was at eleven and we arrived five minutes late. We entered the hospital through a different door than usual (Mom said it was a short cut) and Mom and I walked fast because we knew we were late. We climbed several flights of stairs in the older part of the building and finally came to a stop at the doctor's office door. She knocked and a loud, authoritative-sounding voice said, "Come in."

27

We went in and the first thing the doctor said to us was, "You're late." He didn't look happy. He was an older man with a bald head, pot belly and thick spectacles. I noticed he had war pictures on his walls. In one, he was standing with a group of soldiers in a desert. In another, he was standing beside a tank, and in yet another he was holding a British flag with two other men. On the far wall of his office, he had a long saber sword in a sheath.

My mother said, "Good morning, Doctor," but he did not reply.

So we sat down and waited. I started to get impatient with sitting there while he was reading my file, so I got up and wandered over to get a better look at his sword. Before I had gone a few feet this man barked at me and said, "Back in your seat, young lad." I didn't like that tone. It was not "if you please," it was a command. I looked at my mom and her face was white. I think she was angry at the attitude this doctor exhibited, especially to her son. I deliberately turned, as gradually as I could, while stopping to take a long look at another one of his war pictures, then slowly walked back to my chair, stretched my body to waste more time and finally sat down.

As he continued to ignore us and read the file, I knew this was going to be a bad appointment day. After about ten minutes of reading, he looked up and began to say something but I quickly interrupted.

"I have to go to the washroom," I said.

"Surely you can hold it for a few minutes," the doctor replied, peevishly.

"No," I said, "I was holding it all through that time you were reading my file and I can't hold it anymore."

"All right," he said, "but be quick about it."

I then turned to my mother and said, "Can you come with me because I don't know this place and I could get lost."

I smiled as soon as I got out of his office. My mom looked at me and said, "What are you smiling for?"

I said, "I don't have to go to the washroom and I

don't like that person."

Well, then she smiled as well and said the doctor could have been a little more courteous.

I said, "That's for sure!" Then I said, "Let's go home and we can come back in another three months and visit the nice lady doctor."

My mom would have none of that. She said, "You've had your joke but now we want to get the doctor's comments about you."

I said I didn't want his comments and if he told me to do something, I wouldn't do it.

"That's enough," she said sharply, and we walked back into the office.

I entered first without knocking and caught him twiddling his thumbs as he was looking out the window. I said, "It's a bad day out today with all the rain." He looked at me with a stern face and didn't reply. He then waited for Mom and me to sit down.

He then said, "Here, lad, stand over here so I can take some measurements." I thought about that for a minute. I thought his eyes were going to pop out of his head because I didn't react immediately.

Just as he was going to say something, I got up slowly and strolled over to the place he had pointed to. He directed me onto the scale and took my weight and height. He led me back to his chair where he sat down and took my standing blood pressure. He listened to my heart, asked me to cough and checked my lungs. Then he took my pulse. His last test was strange because I had not experienced it before. He ran a stick on the sole of my foot, and it made my foot twinge. (Babinski's reflex is a neurological test. It tests to see if the great toe flexes toward the top of the foot and the other toes fan out after the sole of the foot has been firmly stroked.) When I asked him what that test was, he ignored me.

I seated myself again, and after a few minutes of silence, the doctor started to talk to my mother. As usual, except for with the lady doctor, I sat in the room and listened while they talked about me in front of me—as if I wasn't there. I hated this! I could answer a number of the questions he put to my mother, but I was Mr. Zero in the office. I couldn't hear, couldn't see, couldn't speak and definitely was not intelligent enough to understand, let alone speak to a doctor.

So eventually I had had enough, and when he asked about urine testing for sugar content, I broke right in and told him that the measuring of urine for blood sugar levels was useless. All of a sudden I got his attention but not because I had said something noteworthy. Rather, he was upset that I should be so impudent as to interrupt his grand monologue to my mother. So he told me, in an impatient tone, to be quiet while he was speaking.

He was going to go on when I said, "I've got personal proof that urine tests don't work." He looked at me sternly but I didn't care. I continued talking about the day I watched my urine test bubbling on the stove. I'd put one inch of blue Benedict's solution in a test tube with ten drops of urine and boiled it in a small pot until the solution changed color. Although I felt quite weak and hungry, the urine test turned bright orange.

"Orange is supposed to mean my blood sugar is high," I said, "but in fact, my blood sugar was so low that I had to turn and hold onto the table to keep from falling. Then I called for my mom and she knew right away what was going on and gave me some sugar water to drink."

I stared at the doctor and waited for a response. He turned to my mother, so I knew he was going to ignore me again. So I continued with my story as his face grew red and I thought the blood vessels in his forehead were going to pop.

I said, "What I do now is, if I feel the slightest bit not right and my urine test shows orange, I just let the pot boil. Soon the orange-colored liquid in the test tube begins to boil as well. Finally it shoots out the end of the test tube—which is kind of fun—onto the stove, where I have a couple of dish towels to soak up the proof before my mom and any doctor that might ask that the test is wrong." I smiled sweetly at him as I thought; I should be congratulated for my ingenious thinking.

Finally I had his full, undivided, angry attention.

"You're being a nuisance," he said sharply, "and deliberately prolonging the appointment with your selfish antics." He went on to say, sternly, that quite possibly the orange test was correct and my mother and I had misread what was going on. I looked at mom and I could tell she didn't like that comment. In any case, he continued, "It's a poor worker who blames his tools for his bad results." My mom by now was stone-faced, and I was sure she was biting her lower lip so she wouldn't say something she would regret later.

Then he said, "Actually this leads to the very point I wanted to speak to you about today, Mrs. Beriault. I have read your son's file, and from all appearances, he seems to be doing well. My measures today agree with previous anatomical, neurological and physiological measures performed earlier. He is above average in weight and height and has a strong heart.

"However, your three-month blood tests here at the hospital have not measured in the normal range for blood sugar or even close to the normal range over the past year. Possibly boiling the tests out of the test tube and onto the stove might provide some insight as to what is going on." This time he deliberately turned his eyes to me in triumph and said, "What do you say to that?" I just stared at him because I didn't care what he said, nor did I want to stay in this dumb war museum of an office.

He continued, "For example, over the past year, his blood sugars have tested 320, 280, 300, 310 mg/ml. As you know, normal blood sugar measures run between 80 to 120 mg/ml. This means he has been measured consistently at almost three times normal."

My mother's face went white, and then I saw a tear in her eye. I said, "Enough!" I quickly moved around the right side of his desk and kicked him in his left calf muscle as hard as I could.

He had a look of shocked surprise on his face and yelled, "What are you doing, you little beggar?" He turned to get me, but when he did, I landed a powerful kick on his right shin bone, which must have really hurt because it hurt my toes in my leather shoe. "Damn it!" he shouted. Then I took off out the door.

I ran down the hallway to the first corridor and hid myself in the corner. I waited a couple of minutes and then peeked out to see if I was being followed. I could see the doctor's open door down the hallway but I couldn't see anyone looking for me. I waited to see what would happen.

A nurse saw me peeking around the corner and asked, "Hey, little guy, do you need any help?"

"No," I responded. I told her I was playing hide and seek with a friend.

She smiled and said, "Have a good time."

My mother came out of the doctor's office and looked both ways down the hallway. I caught her eye by waving to her from the corner. She came down the hallway and, when she reached me, she took my hand and led me out of the hospital. She didn't say anything to me for a while. I thought the bus would never arrive and I didn't like my mother's silence. Finally the bus came and we climbed aboard.

We took a seat at the back of the bus. I sat down beside her and she let out a gasp of air that she seemed to have been holding inside of her. Then she appeared to relax and got more comfortable in the seat. Finally she turned to me and said, "When have I ever taught you to kick or hurt people? You can't do things like that, especially to a doctor, or anyone else for that matter. Your behavior was atrocious and I want you to write a letter of apology to the doctor for what you did."

"But, Mom," I said, "he was really mean, and you were almost crying about the things he said to you about me. He deserved it."

My mom sat in silence for a while. Then she said,

"Your blood sugar measures were not good. But, my little boy, you were right on the money about the urine tests not being very accurate or helpful. After you left, I asked the doctor how we should adjust your insulin if your test is blue, green, brown or orange [the spectrum of colors provided by urine testing]. The doctor said we should check for ketones and adjust it only by a few units, which we have been doing. And as you heard, the results have not been good.

"But my comment to him was if the test is blue, it could represent a blood sugar from hypoglycemic reaction [approximately 50 mg/ml] to 120 mg/ml blood sugar. Orange tests tells us it's high, but how high? It could be 200, 300, 400 mg/ml or even higher! We have no way of getting an accurate measure to provide the dose of insulin you need. Besides, what are a few units of insulin going to change if your scores are orange and your real blood sugar is 400 mg/ml? A couple of units are insufficient. So you're right, we can't really control you sugars or insulin dose with this very clumsy tool, and even a mere boy like you has figured that out."

Then she sat in silence for a while. Her next words were, "We have a long way to go to resolve these problems with diabetes, never mind hoping that someday we might have a cure." Then she turned to me and gave me a kiss and a hug and said quietly, "Occasionally, some people need a darn good kick to smarten them up."

starting lines circled at center ice for the officials to drop the puck.

The game quickly got under way. Both teams were nervous and seemed to be wary and watching what each other would do. As they got used to each other, the game began to quicken and get a bit rougher because the other team had a physical advantage and used it well.

However, our boys were used to larger teams and were not intimated by the rough stuff. Clearly, as during our regular season had proven, our advantage was speed, unselfish passing, teamwork, plus the sheer love of the game. We had a number of "close in" opportunities on the opponent's goalie, but he won the battles at the net during the first period. Our own goalie ("the Wall") was recognized for his amazing glove hand and quickness with his pads. On several occasions during the first period he stopped hard high shots with a beautiful high arcing motion of his glove hand. The first period ended 0–0.

The "Bear" winding up!

Nick – hockey and insulin vials

Early in the second period, our opponents took the lead by clogging up our net with players and sliding a shot through the melee, which our goalie didn't see. Our coach pulled the players back to the bench and stood there and waited in silence. Then the referee signaled to our bench that he wanted to have our line at center ice.

Coach looked at the boys and said, "Well, what are you going to do about it?"

Our guys yelled back, "Score!"

They broke out quickly from the drop of the puck and drove directly to the opposition's net. Their movement was so quick that the big players could not dance with them in the corners, and some of them fell clumsily to the ice trying to keep up. The puck was dominated by our team for five whistles at the opponent's end. They could not get the puck away from our boys and then finally the kid nicknamed Wolverine received a beautiful pass from Lucky Luca, danced to his right with a neat little move and backhanded a shot into the high left corner. We were back in the game.

The boys all raced back to the bench in high excitement to press hands with their teammates. The next line went out and continued the high-speed skating and passing of the puck. However, the opponent's goalie was good and although a barrage of shots was aimed at him, he found a way to stop them all. The contest continued all through the second period with many chances by both sides, but both goalies were playing the game of their lives.

In the last two minutes, our boys broke down the ice with the swift Roadrunner breaking around the right defense man and barreling to the net. The Bear was open on the left side and charged to the open ice in front of the goalie. Roadrunner faked a shot at the net and fed Bear an accurate pass that he whipped in for a score. Our guys were ahead!

The third period started hard with one of our defensive guys, Eastie the Beastie, getting boarded by the opponents. The opposition was going to elevate the physical play to neutralize our speed and try to clog our net with players in an attempt to screen the Wall and get another goal. But it was not to be.

The harder they came, the more confident and elusive our boys were. It was like trying to squeeze sand in your hand; it doesn't work. Suddenly, Wolverine intercepted a pass across center ice and raced in with one man to beat. Quick hands moved the puck right on the stick. The defenseman made a move and the puck was artfully passed through his open legs to the left and Wolverine broke around the defenseman and was alone on the net. With a snap, his wrist shot landed in the left corner.

Nick "Bear" (left – white sweater) working along the boards.

And that was the game. Our opponents seemed to lose their energy and didn't threaten our lead. The Rock scored one more with a slap shot from the blue line for a final score of 4–1. Wolverine was the Timmy Tyke MVP, and our Super 8 team was the first Super 8 team to win a Timmy Tyke tournament in all the years of its history. It was a wonderful experience for the family and for my son to play with such a talented, dedicated and well-coached team.

But now we had to return to the reality of living with a diabetic son. First, Dan, my eldest son, checked Nick's blood sugar using a pricking device on his finger to draw blood and then put the blood on the strip, so the blood-monitoring device could give us a reading. Nick's blood sugar score was 4.7 (the normal range is 4 to 6), which meant our pre-game plan of reducing his insulin injection and providing extra carbohydrates had worked very well. However, we expected it would, because we'd been doing these adjustments for him since he was five years old, when he became a Type 1 diabetic and started hockey.

Dan and Nick had both tested for genetic markers that could correlate with the potential for Type 1 diabetes. Since I was diagnosed a juvenile diabetic at two years old, my wife and I decided that we should take this precaution. Dan's results indicated no correlation between his genetic markers and diabetes. However, Nick provided results that mimicked my own genetic makeup, including the same blood type, and was considered at risk to become a Type 1 diabetic. At that time, he was four years old.

At five years of age, on June 16, 1993, Nick was involved in a baseball tournament when we received the call from the hospital to come to the diabetic clinic. His blood sugar tests showed elevated blood sugar and a urine test showed ketones. I already knew he was diabetic by the classic signs he was showing—frequent urination, constant drinking and thirst, loss of appetite and weight loss—although I didn't want to admit it to myself. These symptoms occurred over a couple of weeks. The reminder that we had of that emotional day was the trophy that his coach hand-delivered to him at the hospital. It seems the two home runs he hit and his field play had won him the MVP for the game.

We made mistakes along the way over those years and sometimes he would end the third period of a hockey game a little bit wobbly as his blood sugar dropped into hypoglycemic levels (an insulin reaction). But these were the risks we took with a very active, healthy boy who loved sports. So far, we had been lucky.

Now that the championship game was over, we would measure an appropriate insulin dose for Nick's injection before his supper celebration with the team. My son disliked injections but he learned to give his own, four times a day, as required to keep his blood glucose under control, plus finger pricks. With that completed and added congratulations from us on his goal and the great game his team played, he was off to supper with his teammates.

We went home and waited for one of the coaches to drive Nick home after the celebration. About three hours later he arrived home. He was excited by the day's events but he was also tired. It had been a long day, beginning at 5 in the morning. So we went into the nighttime regime of blood sugar testing, which had a result of 7. This was slightly above normal but still very good for a diabetic. We decided to halve his dose of insulin for injection and also provide extra carbohydrates for the night sleep. We didn't want him to slip into a nighttime hypoglycemic reaction because of the very busy and exciting day he had had. Soon he was up to bed with goodnights from all of us.

As I dropped off to sleep, I thought of how active a day it had been for the whole family and was glad that my son could fully enjoy and participate in this great day. It was so special to hear his name announced over the PA system at Maple Leaf Gardens as a scorer for our team. I was wishing Foster Hewitt could have made the announcement as I dropped off to sleep.

I woke with a start. I thought I had heard a "thunk" on the floor. I listened and then heard a guttural noise coming from Nick's bedroom. I woke my wife and ran to my son's room. There was Nick, lying on the floor in a twisted position and making gurgling noises. He was completely unconscious and breathing heavily.

I dragged him away from the bed and out onto the open floor. He started to jerk and writhe on the floor. My wife and I knew exactly what was wrong. He was in a deep convulsive, low blood sugar reaction. We were both scared but we knew what to do. Since my boy was convulsing, we didn't dare put something in his mouth (e.g., orange juice) for fear of choking him. So I went to the bathroom to get glucagon as my wife rolled him on his side and checked for his tongue, to make sure his airway was not blocked.

Although I am a Type 1 diabetic and have been personally involved in situations like this before, this was our first major nighttime convulsive reaction with our son. I

41

was frightened and my hands were shaking.

I broke out the box of glucagon from the bathroom drawer and injected the sterile intramuscular needle into the distilled water vial, filled it and went back to my son to inject him. We cleaned an area on his thigh and quickly injected the liquid into him. I pulled the needle out and in the same moment realized what I had done. I had just injected him with distilled water—in my panic I had forgotten to add the glucagon. I jumped up feeling guilty, angry, foolish and frightened. How could I have just done that?

I raced back into the bathroom and opened another box of glucagon and this time drew the distilled liquid into the syringe, then injected it into the second vial of powdered glucagon, mixed it together and drew the white opaque liquid into the syringe. The injection went into him again as he jerked and writhed on the floor.

Then my wife and I held Nick as gently as we could and within minutes he began to settle. It took about ten minutes before he opened his eyes. He did not recognize us and he could not form words, although we could see he was trying. Eventually he said, "Mom," and my wife began to cry. He was over the worst part. However, now he would experience all-day weariness because his body would be adjusting to the shock of low blood sugar. He also would experience a deep, lingering headache for several hours. These were the usual results of insulin reactions.

In a diabetic reaction (insulin reaction/low blood sugar/hypoglycemia) the first organ that begins to falter is the brain. Most tissue in the body, particularly muscles and the liver, needs insulin to allow sugar to be used in the cells for energy or to be stored as glycogen in the liver for later use. The brain does not share this characteristic with the rest of the body. The brain has the ability to feed directly from the bloodstream without insulin. Therefore, as blood sugar drops during hypoglycemia, the brain immediately reacts to any reduction of blood sugar it uses directly for energy.

In hypoglycemia, diabetics act as if they are drunk or on drugs due to insufficient blood sugar to the brain. So during diabetic reactions, diabetics will see double, speak more slowly, not remember things, react slowly to danger because they do not recognize what's happening, sweat, appear white in the face and talk foolishly or not at all. If not treated with sweet juice, sugar water or some other fast-acting carbohydrate, they will have seizures.

A seizure acts to stimulate massive sympathetic output in a physiologic attempt to activate gluconeogenesis – the generation of new sugar (stored glycogen in the liver is released as glucose, which will elevate blood sugar). The use of injected glucagon therefore enhances the natural body process of gluconeogenesis. The brain coordinates the body's functions and when it loses its energy supply, simple everyday activities become uncoordinated. Therefore, the ensuing confusion and discord in the brain results in headache after the low blood sugar episode.

We stayed with Nick for the remainder of the night. After a short while he asked for some aspirins to reduce the pain of his headache. I did not sleep that night, but just watched and held him close as he slept. Finally dawn arrived and I arose. My wife and son were still sleeping, so I went downstairs to make some coffee and call into work to say I wouldn't be coming in that day.

As I sat there in the sunlight pouring into the kitchen, I felt a wave of guilt sweep over me and I blamed myself for the sickness my son had acquired, a sickness he would carry with him all his life, like me. How could such a terrible thing have happened to a beautiful young boy? I began to weep as emotion overcame me. I would do anything to change his fate. Anything! I looked up at the sun, as if some otherworldly force would come to my rescue and save my boy, but nothing happened. I composed myself, got wearily to my feet and went back upstairs to see how Nick and my wife were doing. (Dan slept through the whole incident, because he'd recently decided that, at fourteen, he wanted some privacy and so had moved into a

43

basement bedroom.)

My wife was still sleeping, but my son was awake and looking out the window at the bright sunshine. I walked over and sat next to him.

"How are you doing?" I asked.

He said, "I'm okay but I feel tired."

"Yeah, I know," I replied. "You'll feel better in a little while."

He looked innocently at me and happily said, "Boy! Am I glad we've got practice tomorrow night instead of tonight!"

I snorted and then I laughed out loud as my wife woke up to the noise. She said, "What are you going on about? Why are you making noise while I'm trying to sleep?"

My son giggled and I laughed louder. I said, "Your son, after having a significant low blood sugar event, has informed me that he's glad practice is tomorrow instead of tonight."

Then she laughed and said, "Hockey practice! Is that all that matters in your cute little head, after you scared us to death last night?" We gained some perspective that morning, as we chuckled at the absurd reality of our lives versus the things that really mattered—like hockey practice.

Dan (toque) & Nick in Alaska with sled dogs.

Daniel and Lindsay Beriault

Dan (26) BSc. Honors (Co-op) Biochemistry and MSc. Biophysics at the University of Guelph. Continuing Ph.D studies in Biochemistry & Medical Biology, at McMaster University. Lindsay (26) BSc. Honors in Nursing at McMaster University, practicing nurse in ER, Labor & Delivery with plans to complete her MSc. in Nursing.

Tale # 5
AN EXCEPTIONAL DAY

Teenage years can be exciting and challenging. For a
diabetic trying to fit in, they pose more problems than most.
However, these problems can be overcome if one accepts
the moment and does his or her best.

During my teenage years, I was greatly affected by
the music of the time. This was not unique, as millions
were swept up by the music of the '60 and '70s, a time
when we were considered "flower children." Many of us
used the music to try to express our semi-mature,
rebellious, angry, defiant nature to ourselves and others.
However, in my case, I was not only trying to explain or
justify my existence as a teenager, but also trying to
explain, compensate and balance my condition as a
diabetic. I knew I was different and some days I thought I
had a paper stuck to my back telling the world, "He's a
diabetic."
So my first year in a small high-school setting, in
Carleton Place, was based on telling no one that I was
diabetic for fear that I would be looked upon as someone
different from the rest. I also made a solemn vow to myself
that I would not get hypoglycemic, for this would only
establish me as some sickly weirdo. I tried very hard just to
fit in, make friends and stay out of sight. I deliberately
didn't attend dances, parties and most group events. I was
afraid of what someone would say if they found out.
However, I had a strong desire to be involved in
athletics. Through sports I found out very quickly that I got

46

great satisfaction from doing physical things well. I also found that in our small school, I was better at sports than most. Further, I didn't mind the kibitzing after the games. The sports guys would rather fool around and joke than ask frightening personal questions. I found I could hide my secret rather well in the sporting group, as long as I didn't fall into a diabetic reaction. So I had to increase carbohydrates before football, track, intramurals and other sporting events. I ate in fear of hypoglycemia and not, as my close locker buddies assumed, because "Geez, you've got a big appetite!"

One day, after a tough and lengthy football practice, I came home, ate supper and went to bed early, because I was tired from the intensity of the day's events. I awoke in the early morning to a beautiful yellow glow of sunlight penetrating my room. I lay there for a while admiring how the light put a warm golden sheen on everything it touched.

I made the decision to get up, only to find that my effort to rise was countered by a huge weight on my chest and a great feeling of weariness. I lay back down and wondered what was going on. After all, getting up after a night's sleep shouldn't be this difficult. I chuckled to myself and remarked that practice the night before must have been a lot tougher than I had originally thought! I tried again and fell back onto the bed, completely exhausted.

So I lay there in the warm grasp of the morning sun and my weariness. Time and place became irrelevant. Soon, I became interested in the sounds of the house. I knew someone was downstairs, as I heard the sounds of dishes clattering, chairs being moved and some conversation. I tried to call out, "Good morning!" but for some reason my mouth and throat wouldn't form the words. I thought that was strange. I heard the radio being turned on and listened as someone was talking. Then a rock n' roll song that I had heard several times before came on. The music and lyrics were crystal clear in my mind, as if they were trapped in my head instead of emanating from the radio downstairs.

The song was performed by Jimi Hendrix, but written by Bob Dylan, and it was called "All Along the Watchtower." The words seemed written for me, expressing my deep-seated dissatisfaction, resentment and anger over my diabetic situation and the fear of being exposed to my schoolmates as not being normal.

> There must be some way out of here
> Said the Joker to the Thief
> There is too much confusion
> I can't get no relief.

For me there was "no way out of here." My diabetic state and the needles and regimen I followed were an ironclad, lifetime contract between the Joker (life) and the Thief (death). The Joker gave me a life but in his negotiation with the Thief added a cruel burden for me to carry. The Thief would have to bide his time while I played out the cards that had been dealt me. During my struggle with life, I fully expected to entertain many moments of confusion, fear and pain. In the end, I would "get no relief."

> Business men, they drink my wine
> Ploughmen dig my earth
> None of them along the line
> Know what any of it is worth.

There are those who drink heartily from the vessel of life. There seems to be no end to their good fortune, strength and health. Then there are those like us on the margins, who take small sips for fear of becoming drunk on life. We cannot take that chance. We fear too many things, and that fear is an inherent part of our weakened nature. We are fed but we are never full. We watch as feasts are served but we must only select what we have been ordered to eat. Those who indulge in the feast of life, wholeheartedly and thoughtlessly as if it were their God-given right, are the ones who know little of "what any of it is worth."

> "No reason to get excited,"
> The Thief he kindly spoke
> "There are many here among us
> That feel that life is but a joke."

We on the margin live with the Thief every day. Life is no joke for us, for we are caught within our disease. The Thief speaks of the many but we are not of the many, we are but a few—as if we were selected in some crazy lottery to live our lives on the margin. It may well be that the Thief holds a special place in his heart for the selected few—those who carry a burden through life—and therefore, he speaks kindly of us. It is those with free passage through life whom the Thief holds in contempt, because they have no appreciation or understanding of the Thief or the ultimate power he controls.

> But you and I have been through that
> And this is not our fate
> So let us not talk falsely now
> The hour is getting late.

For the Joker and the Thief, the discussion about respect for life is moot. Their efforts are aimed at upsetting the healthy course of life or taking it away. The Joker applies his malicious and careless actions without thought or favor. Those unfortunates who are snared by his net live a life on the margin, constantly hoping for some reprieve. Those on the margin, over time, become intimate with the Thief, for they are constantly aware that "the hour is getting late."

> All along the watchtower
> Princes kept the view

While all the women came and went,
Barefoot servants, too.

In the opening line of this segment, I envision Parliament Hill, in Ottawa, and the clock tower that is prominently displayed there. This is the "watchtower" I see in my mind. Although princes are watching, and although they have the righteous potential to act, they are not acting. They are like patrons in a horror or war movie who watch the suffering of others but who continue to munch on their popcorn, because to them what they are watching is not real.

We have lost more Canadians to sickness and disease than to any war in which we have ever been involved. Yet the moneys allocated for our defense and security, which is primarily based on taking lives, are a hundred times greater than our funding for medical research and the possibility of saving lives.

Why isn't our country's number-one priority war against sickness and disease instead of killing people in foreign lands? We lose four thousand Canadian lives per year as a result of the common flu (40,000 in North America), never mind the deaths due to cancer, heart disease or diabetes. The enemy is in our backyard and inflicts suffering and death aplenty to individuals, families and friends. Yet our perceived "real" enemies, which cost us billions of dollars to eradicate, are situated in places far away and that few of us can pronounce or spell.

This is why the women come and go, for it is the women who mostly tend, bravely and courageously, to their children, their families and the sick, old and feeble. They fully realize the pain, horror and cost of the battle for life. They know the urgency and the desperation. They beg for more, but the popcorn eaters continue to watch. The women know that they will never see a one-legged general hopping along on the side of a highway to raise money for a war effort.

However, their sick and desperate sons and

daughters must do so for research or life-saving equipment. Our researchers, "barefoot servants," are highly educated persons with skills, insight and curiosity but are reduced to supplicants to obtain the meager funding they need to wage war against the killers of Canadians and humankind. The Joker and the Thief must have great belly laughs at the insane situation that humans put themselves in, much to the advantage of both of them.

> Outside in the distance
> A wild cat did growl
> Two riders were approaching
> The wind began to howl.

Outside in the distance, beyond our wildest imaginings, beyond our most fervent dreams, beyond what is presently known by humanity, hunts the researcher, the wild cat. He is powerful and he is singular. He travels alone with an empty belly, in the shadows of cold and darkness, with minimal resources, going where few have dared tread before. He patiently seeks, with every sense, the beast that causes pain and destroys human lives.

For us, the wild cat has already dispatched two swift riders in advance of its coming. But they can only chase and harass the beast; they cannot kill it. It is only the wild cat that can fulfill the prophecy of annihilation. The beast flees farther and farther into the cold darkness, trying to hide, trembling with fear, but it is to no avail. For the beast knows the wild cat has its scent. The beast howls to the wind in panic and desperation for it knows also that "the hour is getting late."

The song ended and the sun continued to shine upon me. I told myself I must get up, but my body and arms were not cooperating. My arms seemed to have a will of their own, because each time I reached to put my arms behind me to push up, they would fly away like attachments on a rubber band. I didn't sense their movement or that they

went and made some breakfast. I was still very tired, as I always am after an insulin reaction, and I knew I probably would remain so for the rest of the day. My body and brain had just undergone a huge internal shock, and they would continue to adjust to the ramifications of severe low blood sugar over the next twelve to twenty hours. My brothers raced down the stairs and yelled, "You're going to be late for school and we've got a big game to play today!" I had completely forgotten we were playing the high-school football division leaders that afternoon. Then I got worried. How could I play to the best of my ability for my team when I felt so tired?

When I got to school, I went to talk to our coach and informed him I wasn't feeling that good. He said, "What's up?" I lied and said, "I think I might have an upset stomach and I might not be at my best for today's game."

"Don't worry," he said, "it's probably nerves. We'll start you as planned and if I see you not performing well, we'll pull you out."

Not exactly the response I had hoped for but, if I wasn't up to the task, he would pull me out of the game. That was some kind of assurance that I wouldn't hurt my team.

I played with fear that afternoon. Fear of losing, fear of letting my teammates down, fear of letting my coach down and fear that my performance would be sub-standard because of what had happened in the morning. As I joined the team on the gridiron, I vowed to myself that I would do my absolute best to help our team and that I simply would not think of how tired I was feeling. I would use my fears to my advantage. I had nothing else to lose, I thought.

Our opponents took the lead by scoring two touchdowns, in the first and second quarters. I stood by the coach at the end of the first quarter and asked if he thought he should pull me. His comment to me was, "Are you kidding? You're playing an awesome game! Your desire and fearlessness have kept us in this game. Your teammates are following your lead." He slapped me on the shoulder and told me to get back in there. So late in the second quarter, down 14 to 0, I broke for a forty-five-yard touchdown on a "slant right." My linemen opened a hole big enough to drive a truck through and it was a race to the goal line. We were back in the game.

Our scoring rejuvenated the team and we came out in the second half ready to play. Late in the third quarter our flanker beat his defensive coverage and we scored again. Tie game. The battle continued up and down the field during the fourth quarter, and both teams suffered some game injuries. Late in the game with only minutes left on the clock, our coach sent in a play from the bench to our quarterback. It was fake "slant right" pass 14, my sweater number.

My job was to fake receiving a hand-off from the quarterback, which hopefully would deceive our opponents that we were going to run the ball, and then get through their defensive line and break to the sidelines to receive a pass. The defensive halfback saw me coming and also recognized that I wasn't carrying the football. In sports, he who hesitates is lost: he quickly looked up to see where the ball was and, in that second of indecision, I broke past him and went downfield.

Our quarterback saw me break and let the ball go in a long spiraling arc. The ball was coming in directly behind me so I had to guess at its trajectory. With arms outstretched and running as fast as I could, the ball dropped by magic over my shoulder right into my waiting arms. It was a perfect throw. I ran a few more yards but was caught by the last man, the defense safety. However, we were now at their thirty-yard line with less than a minute to play. We sent our punter back to kick and he easily put it in their end zone for a single point. That was it. Our opponents lost 15 to 14.

As our team raced onto the field, our coach came running up to me saying, "You'll have to report sick to me more often, because whatever sickness you had sure made you play one hell of a game today! It's been an exceptional day!"

I shook my head and smiled.

Tale # 6
WARRIORS

For those who fought for their lives before insulin;
For those who fought for their lives with insulin;
For the Warrior that crushes diabetes.

The village had been there for hundreds of years. It carried a dark tale of woe that matched the black lifeless mountain standing nearby. On that mountain, in a large cavern, was a demon that had been plaguing the village for centuries. This demon brought a sickness that affected small children and young adults. The demon caused the strength to leave their bodies and the flesh to melt from their bones. Soon they were walking skeletons and finally they died, whimpering for help. There was no help for them, even though many knowledgeable people worked late into the night to try and find a potion or elixir to stop the demon's cruel and pitiless action.

It was in the early evening when a knock was heard on the alchemist's door. The alchemist was known throughout the region as one of the best alchemists the village had ever known. The villagers were extremely proud of him, not only for his pleasant demeanor, but also for his skill in helping so many.

As the alchemist opened the door, he gazed upon a boy, whom he recognized. The boy was pale and looked tired. The alchemist bid him come in. The boy sat down and the alchemist asked how he could help him that evening. The boy looked directly into the alchemist's eyes and said, "The demon has me. I know because I watched my sister die two years ago, and the odor of her breath is now on mine. It was terrible—at the end her poor lungs heaved like bellows because she could not get enough air into her starved body." The alchemist nodded his head in recognition because he had failed to help this same little girl so long before. Nor had he been unable to save any others from the demon's disease since then.

The boy said that he would not wait like his sister or the others who had been afflicted by the demon. He would not wait to die without doing anything about it. Instead, he would go to the demon's cave and try to destroy it. The alchemist admired the boy's spirit and courage but told him the climb up the mountain would probably kill him.

"No," the boy said, "I am strong and I have not experienced the flesh melting yet, although my breath is very bad."

The alchemist agreed, as the pungent scent that arose prior to the flesh melting was evident in the boy's breath.

"I must go now," the boy continued, "but I need your help. I need something to slow the flesh melting and keep some of my strength for the fight with the demon."

In fact, the alchemist had been experimenting with many potions and mixtures trying to find a solution. What he had discovered with some of his recent flesh melting patients was that a mixture of plants, fiber and minerals seemed to slow the action of the affliction and provide a little more time before people died. However, they could not eat anything else and could only drink water.

He quickly went about preparing the concoction for the boy. He handed the boy a water flask and a bag fitted to carry the concoction on his belt. Then he instructed the boy in its use, saying, "This is the best I can do."

"Thank you," said the boy, and the alchemist gave him a hug and wished him luck. There was a long pause, as both the boy and the alchemist knew they would not see each other again. Finally, the boy opened the door, picked

58

up his pointed oak walking staff and, with a determined look on his young face, stepped out into the night and walked towards the black mountain

As he climbed, he had to rest often. It was very tiring, and the steep and unforgiving angle of the mountain made him doubt his ability to achieve his goal. In addition, as he climbed, he would come upon skeletons of others who had tried to climb the mountain before him: markers of the sorry, brave souls who had attempted the same thing he was trying to do but had failed.

At first, he became fearful of these lonely markers along the upward trail. Then he became angry and screamed to the demon that he would avenge his comrades who were left on this lonely path to nowhere. Finally, he drew strength from them. He would not let them down, he promised. They had not made it but he would. He would confront the demon and, even if he died, the demon would know he had faced a person ready to fight to rid the world of its terrible presence.

His spirits lifted and he seemed rejuvenated. He realized now he was fighting for many and not just for himself or his sister. He moved with determination up the mountain. After two days of climbing he came to the entrance of the demon's cavern. He was tired, but the alchemist's concoction had obviously worked well enough to get him here and still allow him some strength to fight. He rested awhile and wondered how many lost souls had tried to get to where he was now. He would soon set his eyes on the demon that had destroyed so many. He relished the opportunity to face the beast and apply as much pain as he could before the creature destroyed him.

Then he crept into the dark cavern, down a long, steep, stone pathway and into a huge inner chamber. It took some time for his eyes to adjust to the darkness and the smell was awful. A thick, pungent odor was everywhere and it stung his nose with its acidic nature. It seemed to hang like a fog in the air, and his eyes began to water with the irritation it caused. He stood motionless for a time, waiting for his eyes to clear. He noted he felt weaker and his legs began to tremble with the effort of standing in one place for so long. Finally his eyes stopped watering as he became accustomed to this strange atmosphere.

Suddenly, he saw movement in the far corner of the cavern. The demon was huge, approximately the size of an elephant, but looked more like a fly in configuration. It looked as if it were preening itself. It was using its long, narrow tongue to flick behind at its body while it lifted its wings up and back to allow it to reach spots farther down its side and spine.

It had three legs on each side. The pair at the back and the middle pair were spindly and very fly-like. The two in front looked like large human arms with huge hands attached. The body was separated in two parts along the spine by white interlocking vertebrae leading down to a long, thin tail covered in sharp white bones. There was no tissue, hair or muscle covering these bony surfaces, although the creature's flanks were leathery-looking. The column of vertebrae led to a white skull, rather like a human's but much larger. The demon had dark, luminous eyes captured in bony sockets, and a hard, protruding snout.

The boy watched as the creature reared back on its hind legs, flapped its wings with a great flourish and swung its long, heavy tail in a great arc from one side of its body to the other. The boy realized that the creature was strong and powerful and wondered how he would approach the beast so that he might leave a lasting reminder of his presence on that day. Soon he devised a cunning plan that would rely on surprise and on the beast's curiosity.

The boy boldly walked out into the cavern, pretending he was terribly weak and clutching his staff as if he were ready to fall down. The demon quickly caught sight of him and was startled by the boy's presence. In all the thousands of years of its existence, none of its victims had ever reached its inner sanctum. Most died in their beds or on the trail up to its cavern. Never, in all its time, had the beast seen anyone make it this far alive.

So it watched with great curiosity and patience as the boy slowly approached. When the boy was directly in front of it, he came to a stop and slowly fell to his knees in feigned exhaustion. The creature instantly caught the scent so familiar to it from its afflicted victims. He knew the boy was near death and soon he would feast on the boy's spirit and soul.

The demon looked closely at the boy, trying to decipher what was so different and special about this victim. Finally, it reached out with one of its great hands and swept the boy up for a better look. As it brought the boy close to eye level, the boy lunged forward and drove the length of his oak staff into the demon's eye. He yelled as loud as he could, "You will never forget me, monster! Now suffer as you have made so many others suffer!" The last the boy heard were the screams of pain from the demon as darkness surrounded him.

*   *   *

A great deal of time had passed and the alchemist continued to work on finding a solution to the melting flesh affliction. For those who came to his door he could only help by delaying the final outcome of the affliction. Some were thankful for the small delay, but others demanded to know why there was no true cure and became fearful and angry because nothing else was available.

A young man who was well known in the community for his keen mind, compassion and athletic prowess came to his door. The young man sat by the alchemist and they both knew, without speaking, that the scent of the demon was upon him. The alchemist began to speak but the young man interrupted him.

He said, "I have lived a very full and meaningful life to this point and have been blessed with many advantages. For this I am extremely grateful, but now I have been called to do something more. I need your help to fight the demon."

The alchemist nodded his head but said, "All I have that I can trust right now is a concoction I created a long time ago that delays for a short while your eventual death."

The young man listened intently to the words of the alchemist. Then he said, "And is there a thing that you have but do not trust at this time?"

The alchemist said nothing and the young man waited patiently for a response. Finally, the alchemist spoke: "I have been experimenting on animals with many potions, and one has a very powerful effect. It seems to stop the affliction but causes other maladies that I do not understand yet. These include a sudden, unexpected weakening and intense hunger, causing fainting and convulsions. I have found feeding honey to the animals can repair the problem for a while but then it comes again unexpectedly. Very unpredictable! Further, over time, these animals experience blindness and leg infections and their internal organs begin to fail. I have no solutions for these maladies and therefore have kept my thoughts to myself about this potion."

The young man remained silent. The silence became deafening as the alchemist looked away and pretended he was doing something. The young man then said, "I have no choice but to attempt to use the potion. No one else knows I am afflicted yet. Therefore, this arrangement can remain our secret. I will visit here with you every day, so you can monitor my progress and we can better understand how the potion works in a human. However, depending on our success with the potion, I may decide to try to kill the demon on some future date."

Realizing that there was no hope for the young man, the alchemist agreed.

The early stages of taking the potion were marked by many mistakes in dosing, causing the young man to experience weakness and convulsions, which the alchemist combated with honey. Soon, however, the mixture was corrected and the young man felt well and his strength and power returned. And as his strength grew, so did his impatience to end the demon's reign over humanity. Soon he started to work at the smithy, preparing weapons for the battle. He worked long and hard and used the skill and knowledge of the village blacksmith to create very light but strong, sharp weapons. These included a massive war spear, a battle axe, a long sword and finally a bow and arrows. He asked the alchemist to bathe each metal weapon, including the arrowheads, in the potion. He thought, "If the potion keeps the affliction away from me, it might cause harm, like a poison, to the demon." Finally, the alchemist prepared a supply of the potion and a container of honey the young man could carry with him. The alchemist embraced him and wished him well as he strode out the door in the direction of the black mountain.

The climb up the mountain posed no problem to the young man and he bounded with confidence up the trail. He saw the markers of the dead but this did not bother him, as he had an advantage of which those unfortunates could only have dreamed.

After long hours of climbing, he arrived at the cavern entrance. He was tired and decided to rest as the sun was declining on the horizon. He camped at a rock outcrop, a short way from the cavern mouth, where he lay down to sleep and wait for morning. As night fell, he was awakened by a sound. There, at the mouth of the cavern, he saw a large creature that spread huge wings into the air and sped off into the night sky. The young man thought it had gone hunting for more poor victims, and that meant it would be tired when it returned in the morning. He planned to give it no time for rest.

Sure enough, just before sunrise, the huge, bulky creature arrived, folded its wings back on its body and crawled into the cavern. The young man prepared himself by taking the potion, eating his breakfast and checking his weapons. Then he proceeded to the cavern mouth and down to the cavern floor. Soon he could see more clearly and noticed there were large stones and crevices along the wall of the cavern where one could hide. He caught sight of the

his flask to regain his strength. Time was not on his side, but he moved slowly and waited to see if the creature would give him an opportunity. After a while, the weary beast's one eye started to flutter and then close. The young man made his move, dragging the spear with him. He reached the flask, positioned the spear and was turning to run back when the beast grunted in surprise. Its long tongue shot out of its mouth and the froth-coated tip struck the intruder in the left eye. The young man stumbled but he stayed on his feet and ran from the beast.

As a dark cloud spread across his vision, he realized he was now blind in his left eye, and he felt a numbing fear strike his heart. The young man sat on the cavern floor and wept. Slowly the pain receded but the blackness did not. He still clutched the flask and suddenly recognized his hands were trembling. He felt a great weariness in his body and everything seemed to be moving in slow motion. Finally, he fell back and managed to tip the flask into his open mouth and let the sweet taste wash down his throat.

It did not take long for the honey to take effect. Soon he felt better and the sweating and trembling disappeared. The young man raised himself to a sitting position, thanking the gods that the creature had remained where it was. Slowly he got to his feet and realized that with half his vision gone, he had to keep moving his head to get a complete view of the ground in front of him. He still had a goal to achieve and set his thinking towards that end. The beast was still resting but his eye was open, watching the intruder with great malevolence.

With his long sword in his hand and his battle axe in his belt, the young man slowly moved forward towards the great spear he had positioned in front of the beast, the end of its shaft planted in the ground. His plan was to aggravate the beast so that it would charge at him. At the last moment, he would raise the spear into its path and use the beast's own forward momentum to impale it onto the weapon's tip. Soon the young man was positioned over the spear directly in front of the beast, which made no move towards him. Knowing now that the creature's tongue could reach him, he kept his sword high and positioned in front of him.

As the young man bent forward to raise the spear, the beast struck. Its long tongue snaked out of its bony mouth directly at the intruder's face. This time the young man was ready, and he ducked under and then cut the tongue through with his sword. However, he sensed something else was happening when he heard a sound to his left, and as he turned his head to see, the beast cut his legs off with a single sweep of its mighty tail. The young man couldn't believe what had just happened. He was full of anger and cursed himself for being so overconfident.

The creature took its time positioning itself for the deathblow with its tail. The young man sat up and watched the blood flow from his amputated legs and waited. The beast swung its tail powerfully, and as the tail flew towards the young man's head, he lay back on the cavern floor and swung his battle axe with all his strength in the path of the tail.

The tail was cut in two and a great howl of pain escaped from the beast's bloody mouth. The creature had had enough and charged over to the intruder, raising its huge hand to crush him. The brave young man lay prone on the cavern floor, faint from losing blood, and positioned his long sword at his waist with the blade pointing straight up. His last observation was the sound of tearing flesh and tendon as his sword ripped through the demon's hand.

* * *

One day a weary traveler appeared as if from nowhere and walked slowly into the village. He carried very little with him. He had a sleeping roll of blankets, two small shoulder bags and a water flask. His long dark beard and yellow hair framed a pair of bright blue eyes and a warm smile. The villagers had never seen him before and secretly observed him with curiosity. No one stopped to speak to him as they rushed by performing their daily tasks. After the traveler had rested, he stopped an old man and asked him where the village alchemist resided. The man pointed up the street, gave him a few directions and went on his way.

The traveler followed the directions and arrived at a large old house, on the hill, with "ALCHEMIST" printed on a shingle on the fence gate. A bell tinkled as the door opened, and he entered the sitting room. Soon the alchemist appeared. He was a tall, older man, clean-shaven with short hair. He carried himself well but was showing his years. With a quick smile he asked the traveler what he could do for him. The traveler replied that he wished to speak to him in private.

The alchemist said, "Come this way," and led him to his work room. The traveler sat down in the chair offered to him by the alchemist. "How can I help you?" the alchemist asked.

The traveler said, in a low but confident voice, "I am not sick. I have come from far away, from the west, after hearing of your lifelong work on the melting flesh affliction, which plagues your village children. I have learned from other alchemists through my travels that you are working on a way to reverse the problem."

The alchemist was surprised that the traveler knew about his work, as he told very few about it. The alchemist commented that his work was not complete and there were still major concerns about the use of the potion on humans. He felt there was still much more study to do before he accomplished what he was seeking.

The traveler said, "Would you allow me to learn and work with you, to help you in what you seek?"

The alchemist immediately wondered how a complete stranger, with no training in alchemy that he was aware of, could work with complex mixtures and specific measures. This stranger would only be in his way. It would not work.

The traveler noticed the alchemist's hesitation and

spoke as if he had been reading the alchemist's mind. "In my travels, I have helped some of the most renowned alchemists from far and wide. These alchemists have been driven tirelessly by dreams of saving lives and ending pain and have given hope to the hopeless. This is my calling: to help people like you bring a better life to humanity."

On hearing this, the alchemist said, "All my extra money is used for my work. I cannot pay you."

"I live a simple life and do not need much to get by," replied the traveler. "I will find a way, as I have done many times before."

The alchemist gratefully clasped the traveler's hand in both of his and said he could use the extra room upstairs.

The alchemist was amazed at how smoothly the traveler settled into his work and how quickly he picked up the nuances and particulars of the alchemist's experiments. Within the month it was as if they had been working together for years. The traveler provided new insights and creative thinking that caused the alchemist's work to leap ahead at an exciting, though tiring, pace. Secrets that the alchemist did not know before were being revealed to him. The traveler worked night and day. He seemed to need no rest and was relentless in his search for answers.

After months of effort, the alchemist raced into the work area in a state of high excitement. He announced, "All our animals are doing well. They are growing and they are strong," and he danced in glee. The traveler smiled as he watched the alchemist. The alchemist said, "We must now try the potion on me to find out if it might cause harm to a human."

The traveler quickly stepped in and told the alchemist to try it on him first because if anything happened to the alchemist, the community would lose a very important person. Also, the alchemist could then continue the research if anything did go wrong with the traveler.

The alchemist hesitated, then agreed and prepared the potion, which the traveler swallowed. No immediate

this will only be said once and you should tremble with fear at what you hear.

"I have traveled with humans for a long time, learning their nature. I bring you three gems that represent their various important features. First, I present this." And as he laid a red gem on the cloth, it filled the chamber with a warm, ruddy glow. The beast felt uplifted by this warm light and began to relax in its beneficial aura.

"This gem represents the backbone of humanity," declared the traveler. "It combines friendship, suffering, compassion, hope, faith and love. I have seen it many, many times where humans have been lost and alone, in misery, in sickness and in death. It is the structure that, in the final analysis, provides humanity with strength to overcome or accept its fate." The demon was very impressed for it felt contentment, and its wounds and scars seemed to have healed as it bathed in the warmth of the light.

"Second," said the traveler, "I present this yellow gem. It represents the muscle and sinew of humanity. It combines sweat, perseverance, strength, curiosity and intellect. This gem represents man's ability to grow, and to understand what he sees and what he cannot see. It is the gem which drives man forward."

But the beast did not feel anything from the yellow, sun-like glow that filled the cavern. "This is useless to me," it thought.

The traveler then knelt for a long time without moving. At last he began to weep and slowly reached into his bag. He cupped the last gem in his hands as if he were holding a butterfly or moth. He carefully placed the gem on the cloth on the cavern floor but kept it hidden from the beast with his hand. He said, "This is the final gem I have brought today. I have protected it and kept it hidden for centuries because I understand its power and what it can do. It represents the accumulated knowledge, wisdom and spirit of humanity. It is a force so strong that none may stand in its way, neither you nor I. We are nothing but leaves upon the wind when it is released."

With that final statement, the traveler revealed a clear, crystal gem, and a piercing white beam filled the chamber with blinding light. In a matter of seconds the brilliant light was gone, and the dust of the traveler and the demon settled to the cavern floor. Suddenly, the dark mountain sprang to life with trees and greenery in abundance. In the village below, the melting flesh disease was never heard of again.

Tale # 7
VOYAGEUR

Ever had a dream about doing something different and proceeding with that dream, even when others feared because you were diabetic that you were taking too big a risk? A dream that you would have the strength and confidence to step out of your protective cocoon of managed life, and challenge your constant enemy to go ahead and do its worst?

I had read the historical stories of the early travelers to Canada and was especially interested in the coureurs de bois and the voyageurs. A coureur de bois (runner of the woods) was an individual who engaged in the fur trade without permission from the French authorities. The coureurs de bois operated during the late seventeenth century and early eighteenth century in eastern North America, particularly in New France.

Later, a limited number of permits were issued to coureurs de bois who became known as voyageurs (travelers). Famous voyageurs and coureurs de bois were Étienne Brûlé, Louis Joliet, Pierre-Esprit Radisson and Guillaume Couture. They were the heroes of their time and giants to the French villagers along the shores of the St. Lawrence River. By 1712, New France stretched from Newfoundland westward almost halfway across the continent and south down the Mississippi River, based on the travels and exploits of the coureurs de bois and the voyageurs. They forged through a land that was little known to them, continuing in a westward direction, encountering, learning and living with the First Nations people. The Métis people of the prairies were the result of unions between the local aboriginals and the coureurs de bois and voyageurs. They were amazing adventurers, relying almost solely upon themselves to survive in this great land.

The reality of their lives was that of toil and backbreaking work. For example, they had to be able to carry two ninety-pound bundles of fur over portages. Voyageurs were expected to work fourteen hours per day and paddle at a rate of fifty-five strokes per minute. They were characterized by their muscular builds and short stature. Short, strong men in a canoe meant a faster trip and more room for furs and supplies. They did not live long lives, and a persistent ailment among the group was lower stomach hernias brought on by lifting heavy loads.

My instinct for adventure came from these stories. My goal became to somehow see Canada in a different way, which few would think of and fewer would actually try. The other voyage for me was that I was a Type 1 diabetic, and the challenge to succeed at this huge endeavor would be a great personal victory over my constant and lifelong enemy.

My decision to bicycle across Canada was made in early high school. I felt it was unique and certainly not something that people did every day. I also felt this could be a way that I would be close to the land and the unforgiving elements of nature, and in some small part experience, as the early voyageurs did, independence, freedom and the hugeness of Canada.

So the thought played in my mind during my school years until I met a cross-Canada biker in Pembroke, Ontario. I was walking down the street when I saw this young man, very tanned, coast into the roadway that led into the park. He had saddlebags on the back of his bike with a canteen, and a small backpack. He leaned his bike

(Good lord, what was to mind?) They said they couldn't hang around the motel (their rooms were in the motel) because the boss—the uncle of one of the girls—had made it clear that he didn't want male strangers hanging around in the evening.

A small part of the Kama Rock cut looking out to Superior

However, if we biked about five miles up the highway to the beginning of the Kama Rock cut, they said they would get a lift with a trucker they knew and meet us there at about 8 p.m. The girls said they would bring some goodies with them. How good could it be?

So we took our sweet time biking along Superior to

the Kama Rock, where a small park area overlooked the lake. We got our gear unloaded, set up our tents and played with a Frisbee, which Glen had with him, to put in time. I noticed the wind change direction around suppertime, while we ate leftovers from our restaurant lunch. Our fire's flames, with our coffee pot boiling on it, turned from an easterly direction to a northerly direction and I looked out over Superior to see clouds on the farthest horizon. I didn't think much of it at the time.

Our two girls arrived right on time, with cold soda pops in a backpack and pretzels, chips and peanuts. At first we sat around, drank and talked. The girl's major beef was that they were cut off from everything and only got to civilization (Thunder Bay) every two weeks for the weekend. They said they were bored out of their heads and had no one their age to talk to or party with.

So Glen and I started telling them jokes and silly stories to make them laugh. Then we played some Frisbee until the sun went down. We then built the fire up and we sat around it singing songs and telling ghost stories. Both girls snuggled close to us by the fire, as they said they were cold. I must admit this was much better than sweating my ass off getting up another hill on a thousand-mile bike trip! So there we were, on the shores of Superior, the biggest fresh-water lake in the world, enjoying the hell out of our evening under the stars with two beautiful girls. What a life!

It all suddenly came to a crashing halt when a great bolt of lightning lit up the sky, followed by a huge "boom" of thunder out over the lake. We knew we were going to get soaked shortly. We decided to pack our gear as quickly as possible and make a run back to the motel. That is, Glen and I would do the running, while we gave our bikes to the girls to help them outrace the rain that was surely coming.

As the girls took off as fast as they could go, Glen and I looked at each other and laughed out loud, knowing we were going to get the brunt of the storm dumped on us. We began running the five miles back to the motel in the steadily increasing wind, lightning and thunder. We were about halfway back to the motel when it began to pour rain. Our T-shirts, shorts, and socks were soaked and our running shoes filled with water. Our shoes made a squishing sound from the water in them as we ran down the black highway with lightning flashes illuminating our way.

Fixing a flat along the Superior Route

Five miles later, two bedraggled, soaking wet and shivering individuals arrived at Gravel River. The rain was still coming down, and as we approached the front of the restaurant, we saw our bikes leaning against the wall under an overhanging roof.

All of a sudden a guard dog started barking and scared the hell out of both of us. We thought it was loose and was getting ready to attack us. We slipped in the mud in our fright and fell to our knees while we looked for cover or something to protect ourselves. We quickly realized the dog was trapped in the garage.

Our situation was simple: the place was locked up and there were no girls waiting for us. Two large spotlights illuminated the gas pumps, with no other lights anywhere else across the compound. The only little protection we had from the rain was the overhanging roof under which our bikes now rested.

Glen pulled out a raincoat from his saddlebag and I pulled out my army poncho. We moved the bikes out into the rain and sat under the overhang, with the dog barking all night long. We got no sleep. I got a sore bum from sitting on cold cement. We shivered and shook and I wondered if the morning sun would ever come. Sure enough, the sun rose and the rain finally stopped.

At 7 a.m. the owner came out to check the gas pumps and we quickly entered the restaurant to get some hot coffee. The girls were there at about 8 a.m. but they didn't seem too interested in us anymore. I figure the boss must have guessed something was going on and the girls were playing it cool. In any case, Glen and I decided we were in no shape to travel, so we rented a motel room and slept the day and night away.

There were no other storms or rainfall along the way to Sudbury. It was just hot sun, hard work and sweat biking over the Cambrian Shield. Glen and I became partners and we continued to write and call each other after we had completed the Superior trip. I told him of my dream of cycling across Canada, from Vancouver to St. John's, Newfoundland. He agreed to do it with me the next summer. So we spent our spare time planning the trip over the following year.

*   *   *

My return to U. of Wat., in September, to commence the last half of my third year, was filled with great expectations. I applied to be a "don" at one of the village residences. If I succeeded with my application, I would receive free room and board in the village for which I was selected to be don. This would be a great financial saving for me, specifically because I needed the money to bicycle across Canada. I was successful in my application and was offered a position in the following school year.

BSc. (Honors)	University of Waterloo
MA	University of Ottawa
Bus. Admin.	University of Calgary

My next objective was to try and secure a job on the west coast before I went out there in January. I received from other co-op students who had gone to the west coast before me a list of business and government contacts. I applied to all of them. I forwarded my resume and indicated I was a co-op student seeking a four-month placement to work in the province of British Columbia, in

January.

All of my requests for employment came back negative except for one. This letter came from the Haney Correctional Institute in Haney, BC. It said that U. of Wat. co-op students had worked at the institute before and the administration was pleased with their involvement with staff and inmates. They also indicated that they had budgeted to hire three co-op students for the next year starting in January. A position was available for me as long as I passed the interview with the institute superintendent when I arrived. Even better, they paid well!

So I successfully completed my third year and went home for Christmas. I got my bike packed with my gear and on January 2, my dad took me down to the railroad station. I watched as my bike was attached to an overhead sling in the baggage car, and I made sure it was well secured there. I said goodbye to my dad and boarded the train for Vancouver. Glen would arrive in Vancouver at the end of May, because he was a full-year student (September to May) while I was not. I was excited at the prospects of living in a new place, making new friends and fulfilling a dream.

Canada is huge and the train ride was long. Mix in a few big winter storms on the prairies and in the Rocky Mountains and we arrived almost two days late. The snow in the mountain areas was so deep that we could barely see out our windows in some places. It was like you were driving down a white tunnel. Once in a while, however, you would see the majesty and full extent of the landscape. The snow twinkled with the sunlight shining on it, making it look like a winter wonderland. The prairies looked like a white ocean that stretched as far as the eye could see.

Finally, I arrived in Vancouver, where it was raining lightly but was reasonably warm. I found it interesting that Christopher Columbus discovered the east coast of Canada in 1492 and, three hundred years later, José María Narváez of Spain, in 1791, and George Vancouver, in 1792, found the west coast. I went back to the baggage car to make sure my bike and gear were safely unloaded. I carried everything else I had in a backpack on my shoulders. Soon I was trying to wave down a taxi to take me across the city to the east side, where I could get a cheap motel room somewhere on the Lougheed Highway and relax for a while before heading on to Haney the next day.

The sun broke through my window at about 7:30 a.m. and I didn't feel a bit tired, as I had slept like a log. Actually, I remembered afterwards that it was really 10:30 a.m. EST and, therefore, I had gotten an extra three hours of sleep. I did my usual diabetic chores, an injection of fast-acting and long-acting insulin, and then went out to a "free" breakfast at the motel main reception area.

The air had a wonderful fresh smell. The locals told me that, after a rain in the mountains, the smell of pine wafted down the mountains and onto the valley floor below. It was a delicious, sweet, green smell and different because I had not smelled this type of fresh air in my experiences in the east.

Soon I climbed on my bike and headed for Haney, approximately twenty miles up the Lougheed Highway. I arrived there on a bright sunny day. It was a small, picturesque community with huge mountains as its backdrop and the mighty Fraser River as its boundary.

An especially beautiful mountain called Golden Ears stood out. The mountain peak, usually covered in snow, would reflect the sun and make the peak shimmer with a golden glow. As I cycled through town, I noticed an old garage station that had been converted into an establishment called the "Problem Center." I saw quite a few people at the place and there seemed to be a number of people on the telephone. However, the thing that really caught my eye was that they promoted "free coffee" on their signboard. I would be back for some of that.

I found a hotel in the center of town and got a reasonably priced room to stay at until I got established concerning my job, possible new friends and a cheaper place to stay. It was only Wednesday and my interview at the Haney Institute was slated for Friday at 11 a.m. So I hiked around town checking out stores, buying a few items and generally getting familiar with the surroundings.

I also got the local paper to see if any jobs were available in case I should fail my interview with the superintendent. Not much was available except for labor jobs, which I would do if necessary. I returned to my hotel room after a few hours, watched TV, read and fell asleep. I set the clock for 7 a.m. so I could get over to the Problem Center and see if I could get some of that free coffee in the morning.

I got up as soon as the alarm went off, showered, put on my best jeans and T-shirt, shot up my insulin, had breakfast and walked over to the Problem Center. I learned very quickly that the center was a social agency designed to help people with all kinds of life problems. I was met at the door by a kindly young woman who said, "Please sit down and I'll bring you a coffee."

I guess she thought I needed help because she sat near me, gave me the coffee and said, "How can I help you today?"

I said, with a straight face, "You already have."

"Oh," she said. "What did I do?"

I said, "Do you know how hard it is to get a good cup of coffee these days?"

At first she didn't know what to say, but when I laughed, she recognized what was going on and her serious face burst into a wide smile. "Okay, joker," she said, "you are going to earn that cup of coffee."

I could have refused but I felt I might meet some people while I worked. Anyways, I was up for her challenge and figured I would get more free coffee.

So I was directed to the back of the old garage and was told I had to clean up the area as they had plans to expand. Of course, I kept saying things like, "This isn't fair," and "This amount of work isn't worth a cup of coffee," and I had an old back injury, and, finally, I said I was a diabetic! She listened patiently to my silly wailing and then abruptly said, "Tough!" She left for her office on the other side of the garage.

Well, I had nothing to do all day anyway, so I cleaned the back garage. A few people came back to visit because I was being kind of loud slamming things around to attract attention. They were all nice people who were volunteers at the Problem Center.

One of my visitors was John, a French Canadian from Montreal. He said, "Did Molly get you to come back here and clean this mess?"

I said, "Who's Molly?"

"She's the boss of this place. Small, blonde hair, bright smile and very committed to helping people."

"Well," I said, "the lady I met was tough, insistent, bossy and hasn't offered me a coffee since this morning."

"Yeah," John said with a smile, "that's Molly. She's testing you."

I said, "For what?"

John said, "You'll find out," and as he left he added, "I'll get you a coffee."

Finally, late in the afternoon, I piled a mountain of garbage, tires, ropes, pipes, left-over oil cans and other stuff on the curb for pickup. I was turning to leave when a voice called out, "Can I speak to you, please?" I looked up and there was the coffee lady, signaling me to come over.

As I entered her office she handed me a coffee and said, "Please have a seat. You must be tired."

I looked at her and said, "You're lucky I was in a generous mood today."

She said, "Well, at least you're not lazy, but you're also a bit of a perfectionist."

"What are you talking about?" I said.

Molly said, "You scrubbed that oily patch on the garage floor for over an hour to get the stain out."

I said, "I wanted the place to be clean and anyways how would you know that?"

She said mysteriously, "I have spies everywhere."

"Yeah," I said, "you're a regular 007." Then we started to laugh.

Molly became a good friend and I became a faithful volunteer for the four months I stayed in Haney. I soon learned that John, whom I had met earlier in the garage, had recently moved from Montreal and was staying at the same hotel I was. We soon talked and made an arrangement to share a hotel suite and split the cost. I told him this would last as long as it took me to find a cheaper place to live. He agreed.

So, on Friday at 11 a.m., I made my appearance at the Haney Correctional Institute to visit the superintendent. He didn't say much. He asked me to clarify some points in my resume, which I did. He made a few notes and told me to go down the hallway to the administrative office. I was met there by a friendly older lady who said, "Welcome to Haney Institute. We've been waiting for you to arrive. We hope you will enjoy working here." And that was it; I was hired and asked to return Monday for training.

Time went quickly with work, my volunteering at the Problem Center and the time I used to train on my bike. I had been staying with John for almost three weeks when I met a fellow called Barry at the Institute and we became friends. He had rented a mobile home. It was close to the Institute and he informed me that he had a second room he could rent if I wanted to stay with him. The price, location and person were right, so I moved out of the hotel and over to Barry's place. We had a great time together and I met his circle of friends.

Barry and his friends were free spirits and seemed to share a common love of camping, hiking, kayaking and biking to all kinds of wonderful places along the west coast. For me it was like a dream come true. We cycled on Vancouver Island and Salt Spring Island, went to Whistler and hiked to Black Tusk and saw the emerald green lake called Garibaldi high in the Coast Mountains.

Barry and I tried to hike up Golden Ears but got caught in a snowstorm about three-quarters of the way up signal." Oh my God, I hadn't known that and further, I didn't have a watch to give me the time so I could lower it at the right moment in the morning!

One of the older ladies with the group heard me speaking to the man about my problem. She said, "Don't worry. I'll call the station telephone at 5:15 a.m. tomorrow morning to wake you for the Trans Canada westerly arriving at 5:45 a.m."

I said, "Thank you very much for your help," and she said looking, at my rain-soaked body and laughing, "Looks like you need all the help you can get!" They soon left after their friends boarded the train for Calgary and as they parted wished me luck. I responded by saying that if I didn't have bad luck, I would have no luck at all, and they laughed. I'm sure they must have thought I was crazy!

I got no sleep that night. Once the rain stopped, the freight trains took over traveling by at high speed almost every hour on the hour. Since I was right beside the tracks, I felt every movement of the ground and heard the squealing sound of railroad-car noise and the long, lonely wail of the train whistle for miles before and after it passed me. It was quite a night except that a little animal pal turned up.

A friendly, healthy, male cat visited with me between railroad trains. It had a collar on so I knew it was someone's pet. He purred, lay on my stomach and generally enjoyed my company. In fact, he made me feel warm. He would run away as soon as the trains came too close but would return after they passed. He disappeared around sunrise. I expect he went home to get fed.

Sure enough, at 5:15 a.m., the telephone rang in the station for a good two minutes before it ceased. I thanked that lady again and thought what a good soul she was to help a perfect, slightly crazy, stranger. I pulled the lever and the signal was positioned. Soon I heard the railroad whistle and I could see the locomotive coming up the tracks.

The train came to a squealing stop and the

conductor jumped out and signaled me to come over. I handed him my ticket and asked where the baggage car was. He pointed and said three cars down and radioed the baggage people to expect me. The baggage door slid open and two men hoisted my bike up into the car. As I looked around, I spotted Glen's blue touring bike hanging from an overhead sling. Boy, I laughed to myself, is he going to be surprised!

I climbed up into the last passenger car, looked around but didn't see Glen. So I proceeded forward to the next car and then the next. In the fourth car I spotted someone I recognized fast asleep, leaning up against the window. I walked over and said in a gruff, loud voice, "Sir! Can I see your ticket?"

Half asleep, he started feeling in his pocket for his ticket without even looking up. Finally he yanked it out and looked up and handed me his ticket. Startled to see me, he said, "What the hell are you doing here? I thought I was going to meet you at the Vancouver station!" Then we both laughed and shook hands. I explained what had happened that changed the original plan and made me board the train at Matsqui Station.

It was good to see Glen again. We were both excited and nervous about the sheer magnitude of the trip. We voiced our doubts to each other that maybe we had bitten off more than we could chew. I said, "Let's just take it one day at a time." All we had to do was make the target miles or destination we set for each day, and the rest of the journey would take care of itself.

We arrived at the CN station in Vancouver, got our stuff, checked the bikes and cycled down to the ocean where we spit into the water and yelled out, "Cross Canada or bust!" Then we traveled east to Haney, approximately thirty-five miles away. We arrived that afternoon to find that Molly had called the local paper to do a story on us.

At the harbor, in Vancouver, by the Pacific Ocean –
Mile 0.

So we had our photos taken and the reporter asked us questions about ourselves and about the trip. I received a nice gift from beautiful May, one of the volunteers, who had thoughtfully sewn a red warning flag to fit on my flagpole on the back of my bike. We sat around talking and saying our goodbyes with the guys and gals at the Problem Center. Jean (daughter of the famous Canadian Margaret Lally "Ma" Murray) asked us where we were sleeping that night. We said we'd cycle out of town till the sun went down and we would camp there. She said, "Oh no, you're not! You're coming home with me for a good sleep and a big breakfast in the morning before you leave."

So that's what we did. We awoke in the morning to the smell of fresh coffee, bacon and eggs. And did it smell good! As we were eating, Jean said, "Ma is going to call at 8 a.m. and wish you boys luck." Sure enough, the phone rang and we were on the phone with one of Canada's legendary editors, writers, politicians and a Companion of the Order of Canada recipient. What a way to start a trip!

Symbol drawn for me by Rebecca Kaplanchuk, Haney, BC.

Our first day on the road was great and we covered eighty miles to the town of Spuzzum. We had head winds all day and light rain in the afternoon. The Fraser delta, with its lush green farmland, laid the path towards the climb into the mountains along the scenic and rugged in. We finally made it but we were too tired to make any cocky remarks. This mountain had earned our respect.

The biking to Kamloops was extremely scenic, and we got a real bonus at the end of the day when we coasted six miles on a long downhill right into the town. The possible origin of the city's name comes from the French "camp des loups" (the ps is silent) meaning "camp of wolves," which the coureurs de bois named this spot.

Mountain scenes like this are in abundance in BC.

We rested for a while in town and stayed the night at the Kamloop's Christian Hostel. Next morning we went to Andy Brown's bike shop to get our bikes checked.

When we arrived at Andy Brown's, the door was locked with a sign saying "Closed." We both had busted spokes that needed repairing. We stood there for a while wondering what we would do, and then I reached up for no particular reason and knocked on the door. Glen looked at me and said, "Why did you do that?"

rang and we were on the phone with one of Canada's legendary editors, writers, politicians and a Companion of the Order of Canada recipient. What a way to start a trip!

Symbol drawn for me by Rebecca Kaplanchuk, Haney, BC.

Our first day on the road was great and we covered eighty miles to the town of Spuzzum. We had head winds all day and light rain in the afternoon. The Fraser delta, with its lush green farmland, laid the path towards the climb into the mountains along the scenic and rugged

Fraser gorge. At Spuzzum, we camped at a park just outside of town. We didn't take the roadway into the park; instead, we cut across the lawn and put up our tents in a stand of pine trees at the far edge of the park. It was a good camp spot and, if it rained during the night, we would get protection from the trees. We were up early and had some breakfast. I shot up my long-acting insulin (I used thirty-five units of long-acting ultralente beef/pork insulin per day for the duration of the trip) and away we went. The lush greenery left us. We began to travel through very dry, parched, sandy and rocky landscape. We faced our first big obstacle, Jackass Mountain, a very long uphill climb with a head wind against us. Glen and I took it as a personal challenge and promised each other we wouldn't stop till we reached the top. About halfway up we were sweating and cursing the wind and the mountain but we wouldn't quit. Finally reaching the top, we raised our arms in triumph and I yelled down the mountain, "Up yours, Jackass!" We continued on to Hell's Gate and took the tram down into the Fraser gorge. The power and roar of the river were amazing. We couldn't hear each other speaking. We had to go into the small reception area at the bottom of the gorge to understand what we were saying to each other.

Hell's Gate – the mighty Fraser River.

94

On that part of the trip, we had to travel through many long tunnels cut through the side of the mountains along the Fraser Canyon. Our ears took quite a beating in those tunnels because cars would honk their horns as they passed us. Some people might have honked to warn us that they were coming, but most of the time it was a family with kids who would honk, slow down and wave at us as they passed. The problem with the honking sound was that it reverberated up and down the tunnels and gave us nasty headaches. However, we always waved back to the nice people even though they were killing us with the noise. A short time before we entered the hamlet of Spences Bridge, we saw two magnificent snow-white mountain goats walking confidently along a sheer rock face. I thought they must have had glue on their feet to perform this amazing feat.

We camped at Spence's Bridge after doing about seventy miles that day. We were disappointed with our mileage but we had bucked headwinds all day and had had a lot of hills to climb.

At the town of Savona outside of Kamloops, we struggled with a monster hill. We had stopped at a small café in Savona to get something to eat and talk to the locals about the lay of the land. We soon learned that the highway went up a mountain just outside of town. But the locals said we probably would have to walk the last part because it was steep and long. I looked at Glen and said, "Wanna beat a mountain today?"

And he said, "Why not? We've got nothing better to do!" We laughed and went out to our bikes.

As you can well imagine, the locals knew what they were talking about. We climbed and climbed and every time we arrived at a crest, which we thought might be the top, it turned into another uphill climb. We also started slugging back water from our squeeze bottles because the desert conditions, low humidity level, sun and hard work were draining the water out of us faster than we could get it in. We finally made it but we were too tired to make any cocky remarks. This mountain had earned our respect.

The biking to Kamloops was extremely scenic, and we got a real bonus at the end of the day when we coasted six miles on a long downhill right into the town. The possible origin of the city's name comes from the French "camp des loups" (the ps is silent) meaning "camp of wolves," which the coureurs de bois named this spot.

Mountain scenes like this are in abundance in BC.

We rested for a while in town and stayed the night at the Kamloop's Christian Hostel. Next morning we went to Andy Brown's bike shop to get our bikes checked.

When we arrived at Andy Brown's, the door was locked with a sign saying "Closed." We both had busted spokes that needed repairing. We stood there for a while wondering what we would do, and then I reached up for no particular reason and knocked on the door. Glen looked at me and said, "Why did you do that?"

In the next moment we heard a noise inside the shop and Andy Brown was standing in the doorway. He said, "Hey, guys, I'd like to help you but this is my day off and I'm going fishing." Then we explained what we were doing and just wanted a few spokes fixed. His demeanor changed when he heard we were trying to bike across Canada, and his front door swung wide and he let us in. The bikes were repaired in less than an hour at no charge from Andy Brown.

The biking to Salmon Arm was hot over some very arid countryside. I got sunburned and my thighs and hands were blistered from the heat. We drank as much as we could all day, yet we hardly sweated at all due to the low humidity in the air. We met an interesting female character cycling west to Prince George by herself. Her handle was "Snod Southee" and she had worked at Banff for a year. Then she decided to cycle the considerable distance to Prince George to visit with family.

I commented that she might have gone with a friend instead of traveling alone. To which she replied, "None of those weak, sissy-ass city girls wanted to come. So I decided to go myself." Obviously, she was a very independent, strong and determined person. We gave her some water because she said she was almost out and informed her there was a gas station in about five miles where she could get more water. We said our goodbyes and continued to Salmon Arm, where we camped in a farmer's field.

We cycled five hundred miles in five days and camped at Canyon Hot Springs. We had missed our original camp target for some unknown reason. Either the camp signage was very small or non-existent or the camp had closed down. Anyway, we cycled a lot farther than we'd planned that day. We arrived at the gates of Yoho National Park expecting camping facilities there. We were informed the nearest camping area was Canyon Hot Springs—another twenty-two miles down the highway. Late in the day Glen told me I looked white in the face; I

97

was having another insulin reaction. I got off the bike and immediately noticed my hands were shaking, so I grabbed the Billy Bee honey and we got things back to normal.

We had started at 6 a.m. that day and finally arrived at Canyon Hot Springs at 7:30 p.m. We were tired and needed showers, which this facility provided. Also, a nice girl at the desk saw my blisters from the sun and gave me a bottle of suntan oil out of the goodness of her heart. We were relaxing on some park picnic tables by our tents when we saw two black bears saunter out of the bush across the open area and disappear back into the bush. We left all food and munchies out in our bike saddlebags and moved our bikes an extra distance away from our tents, just in case. I kept my hunting knife unsheathed beside me that night.

We awoke to a beautiful day and found Glen's saddlebag had been sliced open very neatly. We figure a bear had stuck its head into the slit and gobbled up the apples, because small pieces of apple were left on the ground beside the bike. We were amazed at how quiet our robber had been—we hadn't heard a sound all night. Nothing else was taken or damaged. Glen used tape to repair the long slit. We went to the coffee shop to have breakfast and learned we were twenty miles from the summit of Roger's Pass (elevation: 4,400 feet) a high mountain pass through the Selkirk Mountains of British Columbia.

Talk about a long twenty miles: it was all uphill from Canyon Hot Springs. Although we didn't see any overt sign that the road was elevating until the last few miles, every pedal stroke felt like we were dragging an anchor behind our bikes. When we arrived at the summit, there was still snow in the pass and it was cold. We had something to eat at the Summit Restaurant. Later we went out and had a snowball fight— between ourselves, at first, then with a couple of other guys and gals who arrived in a jeep.

Rogers Pass – elevation 4,400 feet

We didn't stay at the summit because the snow and cold would make it uncomfortable for us during the night. Instead, we flew down the back of the pass, coasting down the long decline on our way to the town of Golden. It was joyous. With the mile signs moving by so fast, it felt like we were flying. And not a bit of energy was needed from our legs; we just relaxed and let the bikes do everything.

We coasted like this for miles, even outracing big truck rigs that had to gear down because of the decline. As we passed, we would raise one hand straight up and then yank it down in two repetitive motions. The truckers immediately recognized what we were doing and gave us two horn blasts from the air horns in their cabs and we yelled in chorus.

We finally stopped because it was getting near sunset, and we camped in a small park. It was protected from the wind; there was no snow and it felt warmer because we had dropped our altitude by a couple of thousand feet.

We rose to a cloudy day and a zillion mosquitoes. The swarm was very aggressive and determined to bloodsuck us dry. We packed as quickly as we could and hotfooted it out of there as fast as our bikes could go. We cycled thirty miles to Golden before breakfast. We were hungry and I was sure the waitress thought we were crazy when we ordered a second breakfast after a short rest from the first one.

That day we knew we would have another rough time because we were climbing to the summit of Kicking Horse Pass (elevation: 5,339 feet), one thousand feet higher than Rogers Pass. The pass was first explored in 1858 by an expedition led by Captain John Palliser; it and the adjacent Kicking Horse River were given their names after a member of the expedition was kicked by his horse while exploring the region.

This pass was more abrupt in its ascent: hard, short elevations with flat road for a while, followed by another elevation, and another flat stretch. It felt as if we were climbing a giant staircase to the summit. This climb was much more tiring and, further, we had less available oxygen in the air to breathe. We had to rest several times on the way up because we were weary and our legs were rubbery. To make sure I wasn't sliding into a diabetic reaction (hypoglycemia), I would squeeze some liquid honey out of my Billy Bee bottle at each rest break we took. Soon Glen was asking for a shot of honey as well as he was tiring also.

With determination and spirit we made it to the summit of Kicking Horse Pass. It was very cold and snow was piled high everywhere. Since it was dusk, we decided to stay at the Wapta Lake Lodge at the top of the summit for the night. We went to our rooms and showered and slept for a couple of hours. We were really hungry but the sign on the door said the restaurant was closed. So we decided that we would go down to the bar and fill our bellies with soda pop or juice.

Sitting in snow at the summit of Kicking Horse Pass –
elevation: 5,339 feet

As we were going to the bar, we saw a group of employees in the restaurant. Glen decided to stick his head in and said, "Can we buy that pie on the counter?"

The waitress said, "I'll have to ask the manager."

So the manager came out to check us out. He said, "You want a whole pie?"

We told him we had had breakfast that morning in Golden and cycled all day to reach the summit at Kicking Horse.

"Well, gentlemen," he said, "that deserves a supper on us." We had a great late supper and we didn't have to pay, but we left the waitress a good tip.

I looked out the window of the hotel when we woke up. It was dark and raining. I went outside to check the temperature and it was so cold I could see my breath. We went down to have breakfast. The manager came over to us and said, "It's a pretty bad day to be biking. Why don't you stay in your rooms on us and you can leave tomorrow? We were very tempted to take his offer but we wanted to see Banff and camp in Canmore that night. Also, we would leave the province of BC and enter Alberta that day, a big milestone for us to achieve. So we declined the nice offer and proceeded down from Kicking Horse Pass at great speed but with maximum cold and wetness. The mountain scenery was absolutely gorgeous, but passing the crashing streams along the road was like passing an open freezer door. We shivered as we rode by because they were glacier-fed, and the cold radiated out onto the road when we came upon them. Around noon the rain stopped and the sun started to come out. Soon we crossed the Great Divide, where all rivers flowed in an easterly direction instead of westerly. However, there was one exception and that was the Divide River, which branches into two rivers, one going west and the other to the east. I guess it couldn't make up its mind.

Glacier-fed creeks send shivers over your body as you pass on the road.

As we cycled towards Banff, we came upon the Bow River; the water was very clear and had a beautiful aqua green color. We stopped to view the river and saw great quantities of trout swimming in the crystal-clear water. A little farther up the road, four deer were grazing right by the roadside and we stopped our bikes and watched. We were no more than fifteen feet from them, yet they didn't seem alarmed or afraid of our presence.

We followed the Bow River right into Banff, the largest town in Banff National Park in the Alberta Rockies. At 4,800 feet, it is the town with the highest elevation in Canada. We cycled up to the grand old Banff Springs Hotel to have coffee and take in the view of the rugged mountains—Rundle, Cascade and Norquay.

We then cycled over to Sulphur Mountain, passing Banff Hot Springs, where many people had gathered to swim and soak in the hot mineral water. At Sulphur Mountain, we took the gondola ride to the top and got a grand view of the Rockies. We were hustled aggressively by mountain goats looking for free handouts. If you didn't produce food for them they would push you or give you a gentle head butt to smarten you up. We returned down in the gondola and cycled over to the Bow River, where we sat in the grass and watched the Bow Falls tumble and crash over the rock precipice. It was a nice, relaxing afternoon.

Returning to the road, our next camping spot was Canmore and the home of the Three Sisters Mountains. Here we left the Rocky Mountains behind us and entered the foothills; farther on were the western prairies. It was very cold that night and we put on our sweatpants, three T-shirts and our sweat tops and crawled into our sleeping bags. We shivered most of the night and woke up late in the morning for breakfast.

We headed down the old two-lane Trans-Canada Highway because the police wouldn't let us travel on the new four-lane highway to Calgary. We cycled for a while and then came upon a six-mile section of the road that was under construction. We could not bike on this section because it was covered with long stretches of sand and loose gravel. After six miles of walking, we climbed back on our bikes and cycled up the first hill to discover the Hollow Wood Restaurant near Cochrane, Alberta.

As usual, we were hungry and tired, so we pulled into the restaurant for a break. The first thing we heard as we entered was, "Hey, young fellas, where do you hail from?"

We looked over at an older man with a big white beard and a cowboy hat. We replied we were coming from Vancouver and headed for St. John's, Newfoundland.

"Dang," he says, "all that way on a bicycle?" Before we could answer he yelled out, "Hey Lisa, come on out and get these young fellas some grub."

Out walked this young woman, who was very hard not to look at, and the old man said, "This is my granddaughter Lisa."

"Hey guys," she called out. "Do you want a menu?"

"Sure," we said.

We soon found that this young woman was not only physically attractive but a joker with a big smile and a mathematics major in her fourth year at the University of Calgary. She made us laugh until we cried. Since we were the only customers at that time, we received her undivided attention.

We told her about our trip and she listened intently, while Grandpa also cocked an ear. She thought we were brave adventurers and a good example of Canadian spirit. We both fell in love with her right there. It was very hard to leave the restaurant but we wanted to be in Calgary by the evening. We said our goodbyes and Grandpa said, "Young fellas like you don't come by here very often. Good luck!" We left Lisa a big tip hidden under one of the plates.

My brother Mike lived in Calgary so we stayed with him for two days to rest and relax before moving onto the prairies. We got to play some basketball in the morning, then touch football in the afternoon and ping-pong in the evening with my brother's different assortment of friends. Later in the evening, Glen complained of a sore ankle from an earlier ankle injury he had had. Good thing we rested for a couple of days, as he seemed better on the day we started our bike trip to Bassano.

We hadn't travel more than fifteen miles from Calgary when I thought I heard a gunshot. At the same time, I went head over heels over the front of my bike and down into a ditch. I soon realized that the noise I heard was 70 pounds per square inch of air pressure blowing out of my punctured front tire. Glen came back to see if I was okay and I told him nothing was broken but I had some cuts and scrapes. He said, "You're a lucky guy!"

I looked at him and asked, "How do you figure that?"

He said, "Look up the road."

Sure enough, I saw a full service gas station approximately sixty yards ahead of us. I certainly was lucky because it would be very easy to fix a flat there instead of in the middle of nowhere. We slept in a field just outside Bassano that night.

We were in rolling flatland now and could no longer see the mountains behind us. With a good westerly wind blowing behind us, we arrived at Medicine Hat in excellent time. The name Medicine Hat comes from a legend that tells of a battle long ago between the Blackfeet and the Cree in which a retreating medicine man lost his headdress in the South Saskatchewan River.

We searched out the Medicine Hat Hostel, which was a great facility with hot showers and soft beds. We awoke early and looked outside to see dark clouds and trees blowing in the wind. The hostel offered us breakfast, which was very plentiful, varied and prepared by volunteers from the community. We stepped out into cold weather and gusting easterly winds. At least it wasn't raining but we both knew we would end up wet that day. We passed into the province of Saskatchewan and bid goodbye to Alberta.

We had covered one thousand miles.

Saskatchewan was formed from a giant lake bottom and historical glacier action. It was really flat and we could swear, as the vista stretched out before us to the horizon that we were on a giant land sea. The headwinds were very bad and we felt like we were dragging anchors again off the ends of our bikes all day.

The prairies are wide open as far as the eye can see.

The beauty of climbing a mountain was knowing somewhere ahead of you was the crest of the summit, a goal, a place where the torture to your muscles ends. But fighting the wind can break your spirit. There is no foreseeable end in sight. It's always there and you struggle all the time to keep your bike moving. Even going down hills is of no benefit, as the wind won't let you coast down the decline. It was a very tough day on the road. Further, Glen announced that his ankle was hurting so badly that he would have to stop and hitchhike into Maple Creek to go to the hospital. I taped Glen's ankle using the sports medicine knowledge that I had learned at U. of Wat. the previous term. I decided to continue to cycle to Maple Creek and see him there.

The bike trip to Maple Creek was quite a challenge. The strong headwinds continued and soon I was soaked by heavy, blowing rain. This, however, was not as bad as being hit with downbursts of hail driven by a strong wind. This hail caught me completely by surprise and stung like hell, bouncing off my head and upper shoulders and hitting bare skin on my thighs. There was nowhere to hide, so I just had to take it. Wearing a raincoat was no help, as it would blow in every direction—including in my face—and act like a sail, slowing me down as the wind got caught in it.

Also, we found by experience that you get wetter wearing a raincoat because your body heat is trapped and you're working at a very high level of energy. When you pull your raincoat off at the end of the storm, you are soaking wet from your own sweat, which collects under the raincoat. So for these reasons we just accepted wearing our sweatshirts with hoods, T-shirts and shorts through storms and then air dry as we biked after the storm. We were generating so much body heat from working that it took no time for our stuff to dry out.

The work was very hard and I eventually slid into a diabetic reaction. I realized what was happening when I looked up the highway and saw double lines on a single line stretch, one not as straight as the other. Also, it became very hard to push the pedals to keep my speed against the wind. I got off the bike and had to put it down on the ground or else the wind would have blown it over. I reached in my back saddlebag with shaking hands to get my Billy Bee.

So I sat on the edge of the highway taking my honey and gulping water from my canteen. I rested about half an hour, in the gusting wind and rain, and then got going again. I felt tired from the low blood sugar event but I figured I only had about ten miles to go to reach Maple

Creek. Arriving there, I saw Glen standing at the gas station. He informed me that the doctor was impressed with my bandaging of his ankle. The doctor's comment was, "Somebody really knew what they were doing!" I wished my sports medicine professor could have been there to hear that.

We pitched camp at an RV park. The wind continued through the night and it started to rain just at sunrise. Our stuff was soaking wet, so we had to use the park laundromat to dry everything out. While our clothes were drying, we ran over to the restaurant for breakfast. As we left the restaurant, the wind was moaning in the trees and the sky was black. We weren't getting any breaks from this weather. However, we didn't complain and just accepted our fate. We left the cover of trees at the park and finally felt the full force of the wind on the open highway.

Every pedal stroke was a battle. Our legs were tired so we rested, walked, cycled and rested. Arriving at crests of small rolling hills, we sometimes were stopped dead by the strong wind gusts. Glen's ankle couldn't take much of this abuse, so he hitchhiked into the town of Tompkins. He was picked up by a truck on his first try, bike and all. The driver asked if I wanted a lift also but I said, "No." The driver informed me that there had been tornado sightings and asked again if I wanted a drive. I said, "Thank you, but no."

The wind was exhausting, so I had to walk.

I had three other vehicles stop and ask me if I wanted a lift to Tompkins and I politely refused each one. I was determined to make Tompkins myself. It was only forty miles away and I knew I had done at least twenty miles already. So I decided I wasn't going to let this storm stop me from reaching my destination. Out came the Billy Bee (I was feeling weak and shaky) to get my blood sugar up and away I went. Incredibly, I watched as waves of rain came down the highway. It looked like a gray-white fog moving at speed towards me. Suddenly, I was engulfed in a cold shower that quickly passed until another gray-white fog raced down the highway towards me.

Then I saw two funnel clouds form along the way in the fields that surrounded me. I was also bombarded with hail every so often, which really hurt. One time, I saw and heard a wall of hailstones coming down the highway driven by the wind and I jumped off my bike and into a large culvert under the highway. It was crazy, but the ground around the area was like a winter scene as the hail came down so thick it covered the farmland in a matter of minutes. Thank God that culvert was handy or I would have taken an almighty beating from the hail.

Near the end of my ride to Tompkins, I was so weary from the fight that I just kept my head down and counted pedal strokes from one to ten, then rested for a couple of seconds and started again: 1, 2, 3 ... and so on. I finally arrived in Tompkins (taking seven hours to accomplish forty miles), exhausted but very triumphant and proud of my accomplishment. Glen came out of the restaurant limping to meet me and said, "I can't believe you made it!"

I said, "Tell me the food is good in that restaurant and that you rented a motel room."

Fortunately Glen answered "yes" to both queries. After we ate, I crashed for fifteen hours in the motel room. It was so nice to be warm again.

Shredded flag compliments of the power of the wind.

Mother Nature blew herself out over the nighttime. We got back on the road with light overcast skies and a westerly wind blowing at our rear. Now, this was going to be a good day— nothing but slightly rolling flatland and a wind at our backs. We raced along, trying to make up for lost time.

Our chains began to sing. The "singing" of the bicycle chain is caused when you reach a certain pedaling rhythm and speed. It's mesmerizing and you force yourself to keep the cadence so the singing doesn't disappear. It's the sound of speed and power— very intoxicating. Although Glen and I were getting worried about his ankle injury, that day he had no problems. We arrived in Morse, Saskatchewan, around suppertime, bought canned stew, milk and buns at a local convenience store and went to the campground to put up our tents and cook our "hobo" dinners on the fire.

We awoke to continuing overcast skies but the wind was still at our backs so we stopped for a short break in Swift Current. We made good time and pulled into Moose Jaw, situated on the river of the same name, around 3 p.m. (The name Moose Jaw comes from the Cree name for the place, which has nothing to do with moose, but which to English ears sounded like "moose jaw.") This was a mail stop and a place to find a laundromat to wash our clothes. We had informed our relatives and friends that, if they wanted to mail letters or cards, to send them General Delivery, Moose Jaw.

Glen called the local post office to find out they were closed on Saturdays. Glen explained our situation to the postal employee and we were then given directions to the back door of the post office, where we received our mail from a nice man who wished us luck. We each received letters, which we ripped open.

One letter was a real surprise: I received a letter, all done in very stylish calligraphy, from a friend called Janet. I found it interesting that she would write because I had only mentioned in passing to someone else that we would

111

pick up mail in Moose Jaw and Ignace, Ontario. I was amazed she remembered, after all these months, and wrote me in Moose Jaw. It made my day!

We also got our bikes looked at in Moose Jaw. Glen had a couple of busted spokes and I had four broken spokes in my back tire and two in front. We got everything fixed, tightened up, oiled and ready to go. We camped that night at the Green Jade Campground, ate at the local café, got our tents up and gear unpacked and went to sleep early. It was a nice evening with no clouds in the sky and we slept well.

Next day, we cycled to Regina, but did not go into the city. There was a long road leading into the city (about three miles), which we decided not to travel down. It would be easier to stay on the main highway, have lunch at a highway restaurant and continue on to the tiny town of McLean. Distance traveled: 1,400 miles since Vancouver.

As we left McLean, we heard of some more tornado warnings and the sky was overcast. We had a strong headwind as well. We traveled a good distance, and I looked back to see Glen a long way back. I waited for him and asked him how his ankle was. He said it was fine but I knew he wasn't telling the truth. So we rested there for a while until he volunteered to start cycling again. I let him take the lead so we could go at his pace and hopefully work this ankle issue out. We stopped that night at Wapella and had our "hobo" dinner, watched the fire and then got into our tents. Glen was not too talkative during the evening and I knew something was bothering him.

The thing that I had hoped wouldn't happen, happened. We fought strong headwinds again that day. Glen was trailing behind, so I waited at the turn off to Moosamin for him to catch up. He got clumsily off his bike and sat down. He said quietly to me that he had something important to tell me.

I said, "What's up, Glen?"

He told me he was losing his desire to continue the trip. He said maybe, if he rested a few days, he would continue the trip at his own pace. He said he would stay

112

there at Moosamin, see a doctor and proceed after resting. I was sorry to hear that and I said I could stay with him. He said, no, he would rather do this himself. I was shocked by this pronouncement and tried to convince him otherwise. But he steadfastly refused that I stay with him. His parting words to me were that he would meet me in St. John's, Newfoundland, at the End of the World hostel.

I left and cycled in sort of a numb haze. I didn't even realize that I had crossed the provincial border into Manitoba and covered the distance to Virden, my next camping spot. I pitched tent by myself, ate and went to bed early. It was good to get to sleep and forget about that day. I'd learned about more tornado warnings and heard that large thunderstorms were in the area. It was 95 degrees Fahrenheit and the humidity hung in the air. The wind was another tough headwind.

I joined two local riders on my way to Carberry, since they were going in my direction. It was good to have these guys with me because we could cycle in a triangular formation (like Canada geese). This way we would have one person cut the wind for a while, the second person would be rested to take the wind-breaker's spot and the third person tucked in behind in the back draft.

In this position, the third person would take it easy and not expend as much energy. However, after resting, the third man moved up to the second position and then took over the heavy work of breaking the wind in front. Even though the wind was stiff, this method of cycling made it much easier and we could travel longer distances without overly tiring ourselves.

The next day, I got up with the sun and, leaving Carberry, the weather report indicated three large thunderstorm cells in the region. When I arrived in Brandon, I heard a big lightning and rainstorm had hit Carberry at 8:30 in the morning. Then, stopping at a café outside of Winnipeg, I heard on the news that Brandon had been hit with a big storm, dropping six inches of rain in a very short period of time.

Finally, I made it to downtown Winnipeg and stayed at the YMCA Youth Hostel, where I heard that about an hour before I arrived, a large storm with high winds had knocked down trees and some hydro poles. This must have been my lucky day, as I had missed all three storms and just had to deal with strong headwinds.

The landscape around Winnipeg is flat tableland, formed from being situated at the bottom of a huge glacial lake for thousands of years. The soil is extremely rich and prairie folk call it "gumbo." The soil is clay-like and when it rains it sticks like glue to everything. Tractors have large chunks of accumulated gumbo flying off their wheels as they drive by; people walking in fields will have large "snowshoes" of heavy gumbo mud stuck to their shoes. It makes walking slippery and tiring from the weight on your feet. The rich mud, however, is the basis for Canada's amazing breadbasket of wheat and those golden, shimmering vistas of prairie farmland.

More flatland and the wind blew persistently against me near Winnipeg.

As I rode on, the landscape changed abruptly near the Ontario border and I camped that night in the forest. I awoke to a hum coming from outside the tent. In the morning sun, I could see hundreds of flying objects circling my tent. The mosquitoes, "no-see-ums," black flies and deer flies had come out to greet me with great enthusiasm. I planned my next moves carefully. I rolled my sleeping bag inside the tent, gathered the few things I had in the tent with me, put on my running shoes and my sweat top with the hood and took a deep breath. Then I unzipped the tent doorway and moved as quickly as I could to break down the tent and pack the stuff onto the bike. I tried to pretend I was a machine and that the bug bites meant nothing. When I finally got the bike going, I left those voracious bloodsucking marauders far behind. I can see why some wild animals run themselves to death to escape from swarms of these devil creatures.

I had left the flatness of the prairies and I was back in forested and rocky terrain. The wind now did not blow with as much ferocity because there was longer any open land where it could intensify its strength. The pine, spruce and tamarack trees on the side of the road blunted the wind's power, almost as if they were quietly absorbing the energy.

I must admit that the prairies posed many more challenges than I had expected. My thinking was that we would make our best time on the prairies because of its flatness. Also, I thought that the westerly winds were the prevailing wind on the prairies. However, Mother Nature taught us differently. I averaged one hundred miles per day through the mountains but only seventy miles through the prairies battling storms and strong headwinds almost every day, never mind losing my biking partner to injury. I wondered how he was doing. I knew he was a very determined fellow and once he felt better he would be back on the road.

The three Western Prairie provinces, Alberta,
Saskatchewan and Manitoba.

Ontario: my province. It almost felt like I was home, except I had about 1500 miles to cycle before I reached Pembroke. I biked into Kenora, situated on Lake of the Woods, a beautiful crystal-clear lake. In this scenic community, mining, forestry, tourism and fishing are major occupations. I had to make some bike repairs, so I left the bike at the bike shop and went to a restaurant to eat. Since the place was full of customers, I sat at the last vacant table. Soon, a middle-aged man, dressed in a business suit, asked if he could sit with me.

"Sure," I replied.

We got involved in a friendly conversation and he told me he was a salesman for mining equipment and his home was in Thunder Bay. I told him I had lived and worked in Thunder Bay during a university co-op session just the year before. We spoke of Mount McKay, the Sleeping Giant out in Lake Superior, and Ouimet Canyon, which I had climbed several times.

The businessman and I chatted for over an hour and then he got up to leave and said, "Maybe I'll see you on the road going to Thunder Bay."

I said that would be great.

Then he said, "Don't worry about the bill. This one's on me." With that, he shook my hand and wished me good luck.

I cycled to Willard Lake that night. I found a beautiful camping spot with long grass and soft ground to put my tent stakes in. I had already shattered two tent pegs (lightweight, high-impact plastic) coming through the mountains. Hammering into rock that's hidden under soil can do that. Luckily, I carried extra pegs for that eventuality. I learned that little bit of wisdom, among other things, from the biker I had met back in the park in Pembroke so many years before.

I awoke to a raging storm and my tent being blown over by a fast moving wind gust. The sky was ominous, with rain, lightning and thunder coming thick and fast. I packed my wet things and cycled twenty-five miles into Ignace before breakfast. Along the way, I passed the markers for the Canadian water flow. One marker indicated that, from that point, all rivers flowed in a northerly direction to the Arctic Ocean, while the other marker indicated that all rivers flowed in a southerly direction to the Atlantic.

After having breakfast, I went over to the post office and checked general delivery. I received four letters: two from my brothers Bob and Mike, one from an old football buddy and the last one from Janet again. I decided right there that the first thing I would do when I got to Pembroke was cycle directly to her house and thank her personally for taking the time to write me.

I crossed another boundary as I headed east on Highway 17, in Ontario's North Country, but I didn't realize it at first. It was only when I stopped at English River that I noticed a clock said it was 5:30 p.m. I told myself I couldn't have done forty miles in four hours, as I had kept a good even pace right to English River. I went over to the store clerk and asked if that was the right time. He checked his own watch and said, "Yes it is." He saw the confusion on my face and said, "My friend, you've just crossed the boundary into Eastern Standard Time. You've gained an hour, as if by magic," and he laughed.

My camping objective for the evening was Upsala. The biking was good, with nice blue skies and warm sunshine. Five miles from Upsala, my beautiful evening ride started to change drastically. A huge single black cloud, hovered menacingly in the blue sky in front of me as I continued. I thought to myself, "Nature can't be that cruel and soak me twice in one day."

"Boom" went the thunder, and the rain came down like someone had opened a faucet in the heavens just as I rode up to the road sign saying "Welcome to Upsala." I cycled directly to the laundromat and threw all my wet stuff in the dryers and sat and waited. Meanwhile, a beautiful rainbow formed in the sky and the sun broke through. I

118

started to laugh. Mother Nature was playing games with this Canadian boy. Distance traveled from Vancouver: two thousand miles.

The next day began hot and humid. However, once on the road, I had a good tailwind and made excellent time through very hilly country on my way to Thunder Bay (TB). I stopped at Kakabeka Falls for lunch and to view the beautiful spectacle of the falls crashing over the hard rock of the Cambrian Shield. Going into the restaurant, I thought I recognized someone I knew but I couldn't place him.

Kakabeka Falls, Northern Ontario

I sat down as this same gentleman came over and introduced himself as Mr. Doran. I recognized him immediately as a person who lived in Pembroke and owned a retail establishment there. We chatted for a while and he mentioned that he was going for a vacation in the Rockies.

He said, "I saw you ride up on a bike."

I told him what I was doing and he was quite impressed. He said he had to be going and wished me good

119

luck. The waitress came over and I ordered. A few minutes later, he came back into the restaurant and said to the waitress that he would pay my bill. I thanked him and he said it was the least he could do to help me along.

I raced with a strong tailwind to Thunder Bay. I had friends staying in the residence at Lakehead University and I expected to stay there that evening. Sure enough, most of the old crew from that last summer was back. It was like old home week with a big party and lots of sharing of adventures. I got to bed late on a nice, comfortable, soft bed and didn't wake up till late in the morning. I found out I was invited to play on a pick-up softball team in the evening against the staff at Lakehead Psychiatric Hospital (LPH). I told the guys I was going to Fort William (before the community was called Thunder Bay, it was two communities called Fort William and Port Arthur) but I would be back for the game.

My plan was to visit with Mr. and Mrs. Robert O'Hara and their daughter Sharon. On a previous occasion at TB, I had rented their basement room to stay for a few months. Bob and I became good friends. He'd traveled a great deal in Canada because of his job and had helped me immensely with the planning of my trip. However, when I arrived at their home, only Sharon was there as her parents were away in Toronto.

I was very sorry I'd missed them, but I left a letter with Sharon for Bob telling him of my biking exploits. Bob had taught me a poem (author unknown) that would often come to mind on my trip:

> I've been around Canada a bit
> Been from coast to coast
> Had all kinds of foods to eat
> From eggs to quail and toast
> Some nights I sleep in grand hotels
> Most nights I sleep in barns
> But Portage and Main

Is just the same
As Halifax, Quebec and sunny old BC
And any place I hang my hat
Is Home Sweet Home to me.

I cycled back to Lakehead U. late in the afternoon. The ball game was fun but we got killed by the LPH. After the game, we all went for a big bonfire and cooked hotdogs and marshmallows. Then I went back to residence for a good sleep to be ready for the Superior route to Pembroke the next day. I departed early while everyone was still sleeping. I left a note thanking everyone for the good time and hoped we'd meet again in the near future. Down the Trans-Canada Highway, I came upon the sign pointing to Ouimet Canyon. This canyon is a rugged stone formation, very deep, about fifty miles east of Thunder Bay on Highway 17. It looked like some Titan had driven a steel pike into the solid stone and split the earth apart to make it. Huge stones lie at its bottom and the place seems to have been only recently created—almost like you could take some of those big rocks and fit them right back into the sheer walls like building blocks. I had climbed there a few times before.

Ouimet Canyon

One time, I climbed on a rock face at the end of the canyon. I struggled up the rock face and saw that its lip disappeared into a large wooden structure made of small trees, branches, mud and moss. So I continued to climb and came to the wood structure and lifted myself up. I gasped and almost lost my grip on the branches.

I was surprised to find myself at eye level with a very large pond; the water came right to the edge of the branches I was clinging to. I got this uneasy feeling that if I were to dislodge any of these branches; the whole thing would drop over the precipice, taking me with it. A beaver had built a dam so the water would not escape over the cliff. As I got used to what I had just discovered, I marveled at what a sturdy, amazing and ingenious structure this small animal had successfully built. I'm sure any engineer would have loved to have this industrious little animal on his crew.

At Nipigon, I met two girls cycling from Minneapolis to Montreal. They said they were averaging about fifty miles a day and wanted me to tell them where the westerly winds had gone. I explained that the westerlies had taken a break that summer and decided that the easterlies should blow hard enough to blow their brains out. They laughed at that but it didn't change the fact that cyclists had been fighting easterly and southeasterly winds for most of the summer.

They asked me to take a picture of them with their camera. We talked on the side of the road for a while and I mentioned they sure were carrying a lot of stuff. Their quick reply was that a girl has got to be ready for anything. I said, "Are you expecting an attack from the Russian Army?" We all laughed and then I said I had to get going. They wanted me to stay and cycle with them for a while, but I politely refused. Anyway, I wasn't ready to accomplish just fifty miles a day when I was already behind schedule due to the beating I had taken on the prairies.

I arrived at Gravel River as the sun was going

down. I thought of Glen and hoped he was doing all right. The establishment there had already shut down, so I set up my tent beside some trees at the far end of the compound and went to sleep. The guard dog did not bark this time, so I figured I was either downwind of him and he couldn't get my scent or he had been moved out of the garage to another area or he had died. In any case, no barking dog was a great dog to have around. Also, there was no rain this year.

I saw the sunshine on my tent walls as I awoke to a beautiful day. I went over to the restaurant to get some coffee and breakfast. As it turned out, the two girls Glen and I had met the year before were not there. The waitresses were older but very friendly and also generous. One of them said, "Are you the young man cycling on that bicycle?"

I said, "Yes."

"And where are you coming from?"

"Vancouver."

"And where are you going to?"

"St. John's, Newfoundland."

"OH MY GOD!" she exclaimed. "Hurry up and bring some food over for this poor boy!"

The other waitress came over and said, "Do you want extra eggs, extra toast, extra coffee? How about orange juice, jam, sausages, bacon or both?"

I started to laugh, as these ladies were sure I must have been starving to death. They whispered as they looked over their shoulders, "Don't worry about the price, we'll take care of it for you." Wow! Gravel River was a great hot spot for hospitality to cyclists, any time or any year.

Leaving Gravel River, I found that any time I stopped on the road, the bugs were on me in a flash. It was terrible, as they would climb into your ears, nose and eyes. I had to keep moving on the bike to keep them at bay. However, the country along Superior has amazing, rugged scenery. The deep blue waters of the lake stretch as far as the eye can see and the craggy grey rocks, boulders and cliffs of the "Canadian Shield" stretch for hundreds of

123

miles along its shores.

It seemed to me that the Shield guarded its shores like a sentinel with a somber intensity that had lasted thousands of years. These two powerful giants, Superior and the Shield, have been watching each other for centuries, keeping a natural balance between rock and water. Sometimes Superior in its fury and impatience would lash out at its guardian and demand its freedom, but the Shield has kept its wild, powerful companion under control for both their benefit and humankind's.

Lake Superior from the Canadian Shield

Stopping in Terrace Bay, I got some food at the grocery store because I knew I would be camping out that evening at Manitouwadge Junction on the highway. There's not much to Manitouwadge Junction except a sign pointing to the north indicating the little town is that way. I got my stuff unloaded and set up, lit a fire and had supper under the stars. It was peaceful that evening and for some reason there were no bugs around. I fell asleep out in the open watching my fire. I awoke with a start and realized what had happened. I crawled into my tent and nodded off immediately.

The terrain in the middle of the Shield was very rugged and hilly. Trees lined the road for miles and, if I wasn't working my way up a hill, I was coasting at high speed down a decline. It was miles between communities and gas stations. In one long distance, I had to travel sixty miles between gas stations with nothing but trees, hills and rocks in between. The rain had stopped but the sun was hot and the humidity was high. Luckily, I was already deeply tanned and did not worry about burning anymore. I passed through Wawa, with its symbolic huge Canada goose monument on the side of the highway. I was told that the name "Wawa" was used by the Indians because of the large number of geese and the sounds they made when landing in the area to rest after their trip around or over Lake Superior.

The wind on my tent walls told me that I had a strong westerly blowing even before I got out of the tent. Yahoo! I had clear skies and a strong tailwind to boot. I was up on my bike as fast as I could get on it and took off. I did 130 miles that day through tough terrain. I came to the mid-point of Canada sign on the highway. I stood there for a moment and said, "Half done and half to go." I passed through the mighty hills at Montreal River and roared into Sault Ste. Marie by early afternoon.

Wawa on Lake Superior

125

My chain sang all day and I decided to continue through the Sault because I still had lots of daylight left. I called Mom and Dad to tell them I should be home in three or four days. I camped that night in an Ojibwa camping area, where people happened to have gathered for a celebration. The drumming and singing were wonderful to hear. I stayed up most of the night watching the activity and marveled at the enthusiasm with which they performed their native dances.

The following day, I met four French Canadian cyclists traveling from Montreal to Thunder Bay. We chatted for a while and I gave them the lay of the land as they headed west. Proceeding down the highway for another couple of hours, I saw something very strange. There was a bicycle built for two parked on the side of the road with no one around. I stopped and checked it out. As I came closer, I heard someone speaking in French from the ditch below.

I looked over and there was an elderly couple lying in the tall grass on their backs having a smoke. Beside them was a pouch of loose tobacco and rolling papers to make rollies.

"Bonjour," I said, "comment ça va?"

The response was, "Ça va bien!" The old gentleman knew by my accent that I didn't speak French naturally, so he immediately switched to English.

I learned they were coming from Montreal and were on their way to Winnipeg. The gentleman had made the two-seater bike by himself. He and his new bride were going to see relatives in Winnipeg. He was sixty-two and she was fifty-seven. I asked them if they had ever done this before because Winnipeg was a long way up the road. He said, "I have cycled most of my life and my wife is very strong. She has outlived two husbands already."

Who was I to argue with confidence like that?

I put in another 130 miles that day and felt great. My good weather ended next morning as dark clouds rolled in. However, I still had a strong westerly and that was the most important variable as far as I was concerned. The wind picked up about mid-morning and then the heavens opened up with rain, lightning and thunder.

I was alone on the highway for almost the whole day and I think this storm was trying everything in its power to stop me. The lightning was very frequent and close. I saw a lightning bolt strike a large tree about two hundred yards ahead of me. It crumpled to the ground like a house of cards. The thunder was immediate and extremely loud. It felt like someone was pushing on the sides of my head.

It was an amazing experience and soon I felt as if I was part of the storm. My heart raced, my adrenalin was pumping, and I yelled at the wind and the rain and flew on the highway with that powerful tailwind. I completed 145 miles, my best mileage day on the road since I'd started the trip. I camped just outside North Bay and realized I was only 136 miles from my home in Pembroke.

I was up at dawn and excited about this day. I had been away from home for seven months and I was ready to see my parents and friends. I knew I would be home that night, come hell or high water. For one thing, I still had a good tailwind blowing for me, so that gave me even more confidence I would make it.

Just outside of Mattawa, along the Ottawa River, a big black bear walked out onto the highway about a hundred yards ahead of me. It turned and watched me coming and I wondered what it would do. I started to slow my pace as it continued to stare at me, not moving. Finally, I stopped and we both stared at each other. It seemed pretty confident and was in no rush to move. Finally, very nonchalantly, it slowly sauntered off the highway without a backward glance at me. I guess the creature thought it would be too much of a hassle to chase me.

At the junction of the Ottawa River and the Mattawa River was the gateway (or water highway) to the great lakes and western Canada. Travelers came from

Quebec City and Montreal on the St. Lawrence River to the Ottawa, to the Mattawa, to the French River and out to the Great Lakes.

The Mattawa area was first inhabited by native peoples who used the Mattawa River as an important transportation corridor for many centuries before the white man came. In 1610, coureur de bois Étienne Brûlé and in 1615, voyageur Samuel de Champlain were the first Europeans to travel through the Mattawa area. For some two hundred years thereafter, it was a link in the important water route leading from Montreal west to Lake Superior. Other notable travelers and explorers passing through Mattawa included Jean Nicolet in 1620, Jean de Brébeuf in 1626, Pierre-Esprit Radisson and Médard des Groseilliers in 1658 and La Vérendrye in 1731.

On the Ottawa River near Mattawa, Ontario

I arrived at the Pembroke city sign at 7:00 p.m. and immediately went to Janet's place, as I had promised myself I would do. I knocked on the back door and Janet's mom answered and I asked if Janet was around.

Soon Janet (she is now a mother and a lawyer) appeared and the first thing she said was, "My God, how did you get so tanned?" Then we laughed and exchanged some conversation about the trip.

I thanked her for her thoughtfulness in sending me letters on the bike trip. I said, "You know, I never really gave those General Delivery locations directly to you."

She laughed and said, "Well, big ears hear a lot of things." She continued, "I like writing and receiving letters even more than getting phone calls. So writing letters to places like Moose Jaw and Ignace, places I've never been to, made it like I was part of the adventure."

I told her I would be around for about four days before I would depart on the rest of my trip. So we would get together with friends before I left. I arrived home at 8:00 p.m. after cycling three thousand miles.

After a big supper and hugs and kisses from Mom and Dad, I crashed in my room and slept late into the morning. My four-day stay at home was fun. The word traveled quickly in the community and soon I received phone calls from the local press for pictures and interviews. I got a call from the Ottawa Citizen (the newspaper of our nation's capital) for photos and a story. The local TV station wanted me to do an interview for their TV audience. All those things, plus friends dropping by to talk with me about the adventure and my being invited to parties every day I was home, were great.

Funnily enough, I had some people questioning my integrity and honesty. They were very skeptical about my having really done the trip because they didn't think it was possible that even a healthy person, let alone a diabetic, could go that far on a bike. So I showed them my daily diary of comments, dates, locations and miles traveled, which I had faithfully written down each day on the trip.

One fellow wanted to see the bottom of the shoes I'd worn cycling. "What in the hell for?" I said. He wanted to see if my steel bicycle pedals had left an imprint on the bottom of my running shoes. So I showed them to him and he saw the deep parallel lines made by of the outside edges of my bicycle pedals on both soles of my shoes.

"Wow!" he said, "You really did do it!"

The four days went by much too quickly. I was back on the road after saying my goodbyes to Mom and Dad. I was weary and listless on the road that day, although I had good weather and hardly any wind in the air. Actually, I came to the conclusion that it was easier, psychologically, to be cycling towards home than cycling away from it. I had to re-orient my thinking. Instead of spending all my previous time on the road cycling home (the goal), I now had to reconstruct my thinking to see my goal as the other end of Canada: St. John's, Newfoundland. Although the whole purpose of the trip was to see Canada in a unique way, I could not break the thought process that I was cycling "away from" instead of "to" something.

It took two days to finally get back into the rhythm of the trip and focus on the real goal I had set for myself. I cycled through the Ottawa region, long home to the Odawa First Nations people, and camped in a field east of Orleans. With temperatures hovering around 100 degrees Fahrenheit with humidity, I then cycled on to Hawkesbury, where I gave my old U. of Wat. roommate, Gilles, a call. But his mother answered and informed me that he was away working for a week. She wished me luck, and I crossed the bridge over the Ottawa River near Hawkesbury and proceeded on to Montreal on the north shore.

La Belle Province – Quebec!

Even before crossing the Ontario-Quebec border I could see the towering church spires housing the bells that ring to bring Catholics to Mass. Small communities and houses stretch all along the mighty Ottawa and St. Lawrence rivers. Cycling this route was like going for miles down a long main street that runs parallel to the river.

In earlier times, when the Catholic religion was dominant in French Canada, it was important that communities build beautiful churches as a part of their faith. So village after village, some only a few miles apart, would each have their own distinctive and beautiful church. The reason the villages were so close together is that in the early days, the river was the easiest way to travel and transport goods. Consequently, land was allocated to tenants by the landowners in long, thin strips perpendicular to the river so each farm had access to the water. As commerce developed, villages formed at the end of these plots of land, by the river's edge. Most of these small communities were named after saints of the faith—St. Jean, St. Pierre, St. Clet, St. Monique and so on.

I moved from the scenic, quiet countryside along the river and came directly into a large metropolitan and internationally recognized center, Montreal, formerly Hochelaga, an Iroquois name. The city of Montreal is situated on an island in the middle of the St. Lawrence River. Bridges are the only way in and out of the island city. I did not want to go into the city proper, so I kept to the north shore of the St. Lawrence. I cycled late that day and camped at sundown about ten miles from Montreal, in a small group of trees off the road.

A typical village church in Quebec

I awoke to a very still, hot and humid day. I learned that the temperature was in the hundreds and there was no wind in the air. Before I had put in a mile, I was soaking wet from sweat down my back. However, my front was generally dry because the evaporation caused by the circulation of air from cycling dried it. As the sweat dried, the front of my T-shirt became crusty with residual salt and it felt like cardboard. The constant rubbing of the cardboard-like material on my stomach, chest and shoulders irritated me greatly.

Soon I developed a red rash on my chest. I took off the T-shirt to eliminate the problem but now exposed myself to sunburn on my non-tanned back. As I cycled a bit farther, I saw two girls walking on the side of the road. As I came upon them they waved at me and I waved back. Then I decided to stop and asked them, in my best French, if they would mind putting sun tan oil on my back. One of the girls responded, "Sure," in perfect English, with no French accent.

She chatted with me while slathering the cool lotion on my back. I learned her name was Anne. "Where did you learn your English?" I asked.

She said, "In Toronto." Before I could ask the question she continued, "I'm here for a six-week University of Toronto French immersion program. This is my French-speaking friend and host, Viviane. I'm staying at her place and having a very good time." After a little more talk, I thanked them both and continued. I cycled to Champlain and camped in a small park, close to the wide blue St. Lawrence River.

The next day was again a very hot and humid day. I guess I didn't drink enough water that day because I got weak about 11 a.m. and felt dizzy (this was not an insulin reaction). I sat in the shade of a big oak tree and drank from my canteen, which I had filled that morning. I drank slowly and finished a two-quart canteen. I lay under the tree for over two hours, just relaxing. I was still in sight of the river and watched huge ships carrying wood, oil, cars and machinery up and down the river. The size of these monster ships was amazing. I felt better and started again.

I was held up on three different occasions by sheep and cattle crossing the highway, herded by farmers and their sons from one field to another. I passed through Trois-Rivières, the second permanent settlement in New France. Soon I crossed over to the south shore on the bridge at Sillery. By taking this bridge, I bypassed the city of Québec, founded by Samuel de Champlain on July 3, 1608. Exploring this historic city would have to wait until another trip—I had three more provinces to cross! I finally arrived at Montemagny and camped in a cluster of birch trees on the road leading to Rivière-du-Loup. The ride to Rivière-du-Loup (the city was named after the nearby river and means "Wolf's River" in French) was hot, muggy and long. The humid heat was really draining my energy. At every opportunity I was drinking liquids and seeking places to rest: in the shade under trees, in restaurants with air conditioning and under bridges. I camped outdoors again but was up most of the night due to the humidity and heat.

Near the New Brunswick provincial boundary I stopped at a restaurant. I was sitting at my table, enjoying the air conditioning, when a tall, well-built individual walked over to my table. He asked in French if he could sit with me and I responded, "Oui." He switched to English when he heard my accented response. He said he had seen me ride up on my bike and wanted to know where I was coming from. I said, "Vancouver," and he said, "Mon Dieu!"

Once he got over that shock he then asked, "Where are you going?"

I said, "St. John's, Newfoundland."

Again, "Mon Dieu!"

We had a long lunch together. His name was Jerry, and he was a musician who played in a duo called Jerry and Jo'Anne. They had been on TV several times, including a show hosted by Ian Tyson, which aired on the CBC. He wanted to give me some of his albums but I had no place to carry them. We exchanged addresses and he said he would send them to my home. We then said goodbye and he said, "Don't worry about the bill. I've got it covered."

I crossed the Quebec boundary into the province of New Brunswick. That night, in a small park near St. Basil, New Brunswick, all hell broke loose as rain, high winds, thunder and lightning flattened my tent and soaked everything. With everything wet, I looked for shelter and saw the men's washroom facility. I dragged my stuff over there and found a wooden stool to sit on. I hung my stuff up to dry and sat down and leaned against the wall and fell asleep.

Me and my shadow – on the way to the Maritimes

In the morning, I heard a noise and awoke to see a small, cute face looking at me through the door. The little boy was about seven years old with sandy brown hair and deep brown eyes. He hesitated and turned and said to his dad, "There's a funny-looking man sleeping in the washroom."

His dad said, "Okay, son. I'll be there in a moment."

By the time the dad arrived, I was up, had a big stretch to loosen up my sore joints and started gathering my still damp gear. The little boy watched intently but didn't say anything until his dad arrived. Then, before his dad could speak, he said, "That man got soaked last night in the rain storm and he's drying his stuff in here."

His dad said, "That's okay, son. It wasn't fit for man or beast last night."

The little boy kept watching me from inside the washroom—he had pushed the door open just a bit and was peering at me through the crack—as I took my gear outside and hung it on the branches of trees to dry in the sun. I walked over to my bike and checked it out. The rain had fallen on my chain so heavily that it was covered with small rings of rust. I had to take my oil can out, give the chain a liberal dosing of oil and circulate the pedals until the rasping sound of rust disappeared.

Province of New Brunswick

When I turned around I saw the little boy still watching. I was going to wave to him to come over and check out my bike, but his dad came out of the washroom and had him by the hand. He led the boy over to the silver mobile camping unit they had attached to the back of their car.

I sat in the sun and waited for my gear to dry out. Shortly, the family drove past me on their way out of the park. The mother and father were in the front seat of the car and an older girl and the little boy were in the back. As they passed me they all waved to me and the dad shouted, "Good luck," through his open window. As the car drove away, the little boy was looking out his window and continued waving till he was out of sight. Suddenly I had this feeling of déjà vu. I had somehow seen this before.

I cycled another hundred miles that day and camped in a freshly cut hayfield just outside Woodstock, New Brunswick. I love the sweet smell of new-cut hay. The camp site was perfect: no bugs, enough soft soil to put my tent pegs in and a clear sky.

Over the past few weeks, I had been starting to get nagging aches and pains. My right knee was bothering me. My ankles were swelling and my middle finger on my right hand was going numb. I didn't know what was causing these concerns.

As I was getting ready to sleep, an intermediate-sized sandy brown dog came over to the tent. It was obviously curious but very cautious. When I tried to be friendly with the dog, it growled and pulled away but its tail was wagging. That told me that it was more afraid of me than I of it. So I waited as the dog moved erratically around the outside of the tent, all the while keeping an eye on me.

After a short while, the dog let me touch its head and it smelled and licked my hand. I slipped the dog a piece of leftover cheese from my saddle bag and it really loosened up and became very friendly. Soon it was playing with me and wanted to be petted and hugged. I played with the dog for a long time, throwing a stick I had found, and it would chase it.

Finally the sun was setting, so I told it to go home and that I was going to sleep. The dog did not leave. As I opened the tent, it rushed in and lay down on my sleeping bag. "Hey buddy," I said, "That's my bed, not yours." However, it didn't listen and seemed quite content to wag its tail and stay right where it was. I couldn't get it out of the tent. For every action that I initiated to get it out, there was an equal and opposite reaction from the dog to stay put. Finally, I gave up and let it stay at the bottom of the sleeping bag by the open door of the tent. I slept well that night.

When I awoke, the dog was still there and I had to crawl over it to get out of my tent. It immediately went deeper into the tent and decided to sleep some more. I had breakfast, injected my insulin and started to pack stuff on my bike. I pulled my sleeping bag out of the tent but the dog stayed in the tent. I called to it to try and lure it out. No response. It just kept looking at me, breathing with its tongue stuck out and wagging its tail. So I collapsed the tent on top of it when I pulled the main support pole out. It was out of there in a flash.

The sky was dark and the dog wouldn't leave. I started cycling and the dog followed. It was having a great time and just wouldn't go away, even when I stopped and scolded it to go home. Finally, a nasty storm hit—heavy rain, then a burst of hail that lasted about five minutes, then back to light rain. When I turned to see where the dog was, it had disappeared. I can safely say that the dog was smart enough to know not to be out in a hailstorm. I can also say I missed the little beggar. It was good company.

That day was tough. The terrain was very hilly and the wind was in front of me, making me fight for each pedal stroke. The really bad part was that even when I fought to make it to the top of one of those long, high hills, I got no rest coming down because the wind would make me pedal down the decline. Work up the hill and work down the hill: it just wasn't fair!

Then I started to laugh at myself and said out loud, "Who am I to dictate terms to Mother Nature or say what is fair or unfair?" I was just a speck on a little rock called Earth, somewhere in the vast expanse of the universe. So I kept my mouth shut the rest of the way to Sheffield. I did ninety miles that day. My knees were still bothering me and my finger was numb again. I camped in a clump of spruce near the highway after washing and drying my stuff at the laundromat.

I cycled 110 miles in very dry weather. It seems that these parts of the Maritimes were suffering from a drought; they hadn't seen rain in over eight weeks. The ditches along the highway were bone dry; the streams were either dried up or had only little trickles of water in them. The rivers were low and brown in color, and the grass was stiff and burnt from the sun. I cycled into the Moncton area. Although the region was originally settled in 1670s by the French Acadians, they had been forcibly removed from their lands by the British in 1755, and Moncton is considered to have been officially founded in 1766 with the arrival of Pennsylvania Dutch immigrants from Philadelphia.

I stopped at Howard Johnson's Restaurant because I had learned they would give you a whole pot of coffee for a quarter. As I entered, I saw a table to the right and sat down. I was looking over the menu and waiting for the waitress to arrive when I glanced up to find myself staring into a pair of deep brown eyes. I knew who it was immediately. He said, "Are you still sleeping in washrooms?"

I laughed and said, "No, I'm not."

"Did you bike all the way from that campsite?" he said

"Yes, I did."

Suddenly his dad called out, "Jimmy, where are you?" So I took his hand and guided him back to his family. The family was amazed that I had come so far so quickly.

I said, "I can assure you that when you're biking, it sure doesn't feel so quick."

I was then invited for supper with them. They asked a lot of questions and I answered politely and in detail. Jimmy stared at me all through supper. We had a good time and I found out they were from London, Ontario, and were taking a tour of the Maritimes. They said their last week would be spent on the "Rock," the nickname for Newfoundland. As I left, I said to the father, "We might see each other again because I'll be in Newfoundland by the next week." I turned and said to Jimmy, "Do you want to come out and see my bike?"

He turned to his dad and his dad said, "Okay." So Jimmy said, "You bet!"

I held his hand and went out to the bike and he asked several questions like, "How fast can you go? Where do you sleep? Where are your tent and sleeping bag? Where is your water? How do you eat?" and on and on. It was obvious he had been thinking a lot about the biking process since our last meeting.

Jimmy's dad walked over and said, "It's time to go."

The kid didn't want to go because he still had more questions to ask.

I said, "Keep your eyes open in Newfoundland, Jimmy. I'm going there, too, and you might spot me on the road." I shook his hand and said goodbye. That night I slept in the forest about ten miles outside of Moncton.

I left New Brunswick that day after a good day of biking. I was a couple of miles outside Truro, Nova Scotia, when suddenly I heard a car behind me sounding its horn. I was already as far over as I could go on the six-foot-wide paved shoulder, so I didn't know what the horn-honking was about. The next thing I knew, the car appeared beside me and the punks in it were laughing and pointing at me. They must have been drunk.

The next thing, the car veered very close and clipped my pedal. I flew into the ditch and landed on my back. I was up in an instant, roaring mad, and running after the car. I picked up stones and threw them as I ran, twice hitting the back trunk, but the idiots just kept on going while waving goodbye out the windows. A group of young punks spreading their depraved version of fun throughout the land!

I was cut in several places. My right leg and ankle were hurting and the front wheel of my bike was demolished. I was upset by the sheer stupidity of the act that these yokels had perpetrated upon me. I sat for a while on the side of the road until an old man in a beat up pick-up truck stopped and asked if I was okay. I said I was all right. He said, "Well, you might be all right but your bike looks like it's taken a beating."

I had to smile and I said, "Yeah, you're right about that."

The bagpiper meets me at the province of Nova Scotia.

He paused for a while and then said, "You can put your bike in the truck and ride along with me into Truro. I know a bike shop there." What a nice gesture!

Sure enough, he dropped me off at the bike shop and the young guys there did a great job on my bike. They also let me use the store washroom to get cleaned up as I was quite a mess, with dried blood and dirt all over my arms and legs.

When I told them what had happened they became more upset than I was. They wanted me to describe the car and asked if I could remember anything about the punks in the car. I said, "Hold it, guys. I don't need you chasing over the countryside evening the score for me." I told them to leave it alone and I said, "What comes around goes around. There'll be a day of reckoning for their actions."

Then one fellow said, "Let's go to the restaurant for lunch, our treat." Well, how could I refuse that invitation? Further, I didn't have to pay for any of my bike repairs. I had traveled four thousand miles to that day.

I traveled easy the next day—no headwind and a gently rolling terrain. Still, drought conditions were evident everywhere, as I saw dry mud ditches, brown crispy grass and low rivers and ponds wherever I traveled on the highway. The heat was a dry heat, which was much better than humid heat for my personal comfort; however, because of the dryness, I would get grit in my mouth from the dust in the air.

The rivers were almost dried out from the drought.

My ankle and leg were sore from the previous day's event and the fingers of my left hand were still going numb on me. The bike was performing very well after the work done at the Truro bike shop. I cycled into Antigonish and went to visit St. Francis Xavier University. Then I went to the Youth Hostel in town, got a shower, washed my gear and slept on a nice soft mattress.

I slept deeply and the hostel attendant took pity on me and let me sleep in, which is against hostel rules. I awoke feeling like a whole new person. My leg and ankle felt fine; my hands and fingers weren't numb and I felt great. I got on my bike and set my goal to get to Bras d'Or Lake in the Cape Breton region. Bras d'Or means "arms of gold"; the French explorers who named the lake may have been referring to the sun's rays reflected upon its waters.

I stopped at a gas station when it started to drizzle later in the day. (First rain they had seen in over eight weeks.) I was standing under the large canopy when the attendant came out to talk to me. After I answered the usual questions, he said, "I can't even imagine how big a distance that is because I lived my whole life in Nova Scotia and a little bit in New Brunswick. I never even thought of going anywhere else because this is my home and it's so beautiful here."

I said, "Canada is your home and it's beautiful wherever you go." I told him he had to go and see the rest of it.

"Maybe. I might do that," he said quietly, "after hearing your story about the bike trip today."

So I said to him, "When I was in the Rockies, I stopped at a gas station, and a fellow asked me what was I doing and I told him I was heading east. His comment was to stay in the beautiful Rockies where every curve brought new sights, towering mountain delights, wild animals seen from the road and water as pure as God's driven snow. Going east all you got was the big flat boring prairies and big filthy cities with lots of weirdoes and smelly fish in the Maritimes.

"On the prairies, I stopped at a small restaurant and the owner asked me where I was going and I said, 'Coming from the Rockies and going to Eastern Canada.' And he said, 'Well, you're in God's open land now. You can see forever out here. There's plenty of fresh air, blue skies, sunshine, freedom and the breadbasket of the world. The Rockies, you can't see ahead for all the curves and mountains in the way. You only see the sun for a short time every day because the mountains blot it out; you're always in shadows. The east,' he went on, 'you can't breathe out there for all those polluted cities and in the Maritimes all they have is fish."

The attendant frowned, but I wasn't done.

"So," I said to him, "as you can see, everyone in Canada thinks their region is the most beautiful place to be. The problem is that few understand Canada's magnitude or its thousands of beautiful locations along its five-thousand mile girth. You must see it to believe it."

The drizzle stopped and, as I got on my bike, the attendant came out with a goody bag for me as a treat along the road. I thanked him for his thoughtfulness and generosity as I stuffed the parcel into my saddlebag.

Later, I met a group of seven bikers (three girls and four boys) cycling on the road. They were from New England and doing a summer trip in Canada. We started to talk and I found out they were cycling the Cabot Trail. It is named after the explorer John Cabot, who landed in Atlantic Canada in 1497.

"You're taking on a really tough ride," I commented, "because it's just up and down biking with the wind coming constantly off the ocean."

However, they were amazed at my journey ("Far out!") and were really bummed out to learn that I was averaging ninety-five miles a day and they were only doing sixty.

I said, "You're traveling as a group and, therefore, you can only travel as fast as your slowest person and can only leave your camp in the morning as early as the longest sleeper. I don't have any of those burdens. But you have a group of friends you can talk with, share problems with, share repairs, food and water with; I don't have these pleasures."

I wished them good luck and continued to North Sydney.

It was a beautiful summer night and I decided not to put up my tent because I wanted to sleep under the stars. However, knowing Mother Nature was prone to playing tricks on me, I wisely put my bike, gear and sleeping bag under a large maple tree. Sure enough, I woke up with a start when I felt rain drops getting through my leaf canopy and nailing me rudely in the eye. It didn't rain more than fifteen minutes and then it was over. I was not that affected. I guess Mother Nature was just testing me again.

At my stops at the gas station, the Truro bike shop and in Bras d'Or, I had learned of a large mountain called Kelly's Mountain, which was on my way to North Sydney.

I came to a sign on the road that said "4 miles to Kelly's Mountain." At the next gas station-restaurant combo I decided to get some information.

I sat down for lunch and engaged in conversation with a couple of guys. They informed me that Kelly's Mountain was the highest elevation in Nova Scotia and that those who had previously biked on it usually had to walk to the summit because they were too tired to continue pedaling. I thought to myself that this was very much the same scenario that Glen and I had faced at Savonna Mountain in British Columbia. I figured I was in for a long hard climb.

I got out on the road and cycled for a few miles and came to a sign on the side of the road. It said: "Kelly's Mountain (elevation 800 feet)." I stood there for a second, thinking I had misread the sign. Then I closed my eyes, opened them, read it again and started to laugh. The formidable Kelly's Mountain was no match for Rogers Pass (4,400 feet) and Kicking Horse Pass (5,400 feet). I biked to the top of the summit without resting or walking any part of the mountain. Then, without stopping, I biked over the summit and had a long enjoyable downhill.

It was forty miles to North Sydney by bike. From there I would take the ferry to Newfoundland, one of Canada's two island provinces. I took my time because I had all day and only a short distance to travel before I reached the Atlantic Ocean. I arrived at the CN docks at North Sydney to find another biker. It seems he had cycled approximately seven hundred miles through Quebec and the Maritimes and was planning to take the ferry the next day to Argentia, Newfoundland.

I was not going to Argentia but to Port aux Basques, a natural, deep-water port on the southwest coast of Newfoundland, named in the 1500s by the French Basques fishermen who used it as a haven in storms and a base for fishing and exploration. Argentia was only fifty miles from St. John's, whereas from Port aux Basques to St. John's was about six hundred miles through the interior of the island. The biker said I was crazy to cycle through the interior, which were just miles of nothing but trees and rocks. I said I had already cycled miles of nothing on the western prairies and the Cambrian Shield in northern Ontario, so I wasn't worried about it. He just shook his head and wished me luck.

The Atlantic Ocean ferry crossing at North Sydney for
Port aux Basques, Newfoundland

I bought my ticket on the ship called the Marina

Atlantica for Port aux Basques. As I was waiting for the ship to dock, an announcement came over the PA telling everyone that this would be the last crossing until the weather cleared. I was curious, so as I saw a seaman in whites going by I said, "Hey, buddy, what's that announcement all about?"

He said, "Hurricane Blanche is coming up the Atlantic coast and this is the last ship crossing till things settle down."

I thought about that for a while. Then I decided that these sea people knew more about the ocean than I did. If they were willing to send people out on the ocean at this time, I shouldn't have to worry. I got onboard and watched my bike being safely stored away for the trip. I proceeded up into the central section of the boat and looked out upon the ocean. It looked darker in the skies now and the waves were picking up. We left North Sydney for Port aux Basques at 5:30 p.m. We arrived eight hours later, in the early morning.

We had a brutal trip over (at least for a landlubber like me). The ship was in constant motion once we left port. Many of the people around me were getting seasick in their plastic bags provided by crew members. I fortunately did not get seasick, but I got a pounding headache early into the long trip. The waves seemed massive to me. I went as close to the front of the boat as I could get to view white storms of froth and waves savagely crashing over the prow of the boat. I spoke to a crew member going by and queried, "It's going pretty badly?"

He replied with a smile, "I've seen a lot worse." He said this was just the beginning. The main storm was still two hundred miles south of us, so we would miss the really ugly and powerful part. Good Lord, if this was only bad, I sure didn't want to see worse. I took a few aspirins given to me by a crew member and waited for land.

After we docked, I stayed in the CN terminal building that night as I had nowhere to go. I knew the Youth Hostel was about five miles out of town, but in the darkness and heavy rain, without directions, I thought I'd better stay put. I watched some seamen playing penny Black Jack and Twenty-one. After sitting by myself for a while, one of the guys said, "Are you going to sit there all night?"

"Pretty much," I replied.

"Well, you might as well come over and play poker with us," he said

We played until the sky grew light, though it continued raining. I got directions to the Newfie Bullit hostel. During a clear spell in the storm, I cycled five miles up the highway to the hostel.

The hostel was made of old CN boxcars and passenger cars that used to run on narrow gauge track across Newfoundland. It was run by the Anglican Church and the attendants at the hostel were hilarious. I slept there to about three in the afternoon, and then hitched a ride back to Port aux Basques to do some shopping for food items. From what I had been told, the highway distances between communities on the interior highway were very long and empty.

I hitched a ride back to the hostel and loaded up my supplies on the bike. There were three attendants and three visitors (including me) at the hostel. The other two were hitchhikers who had come over on the same boat that I had. They were from Drumheller, Alberta, home of the badlands and dinosaurs. They had been on the road for six weeks and Newfoundland was their last destination to visit before they headed home by train. The group of us settled down, two of the attendants played some guitar for us, and we talked about where we were from and what we were doing in our travels.

Someone was listening to the radio and informed us that Hurricane Blanche had arrived at the Bay of Fundy, in Nova Scotia, and was expected to blow into Newfoundland by the next day. However, the radio report said the hurricane had been downgraded to major storm status. I liked the sound of that, but we could still feel the wind pushing on the train cars as we sat and talked. I went to bed at approximately midnight and awoke in the morning to the train car being pushed by a strong gust of wind.

I got up and went outside to check my bike (it was blown down during the night) and to gauge the weather. It was not raining at that moment, but the wind was fast. I realized, however, that the wind was in a northeast direction and that translated into a powerful tailwind for me. I decided I had to get on the road and take advantage of this sweet development. Besides, I would have the help of the wind as I cycled into mountainous terrain—the Long Range Mountains—along the coast.

Approximately thirty miles up the coast, with the wind pushing me at a tremendous pace up and down hills, I came to the "Wreck House Stretch." At this point, the geography of the Long Range Mountains can form a funnel for winds coming off the Atlantic. If the weather conditions and angle of the wind are just right, the Atlantic wind is funneled and can blow houses, cars, trucks and railroad trains over. Luckily, although the wind was powerful, I did not experience any crosswinds coming from the ocean—a good thing, because those funnel winds apparently traveled at 120 miles per hour. However, I was blown sideways on my bike twice without incident when the highway curved away from the wind flow and my tailwind became a crosswind. Lifted by the wind, I felt like I was floating as I caught myself from falling.

The world was moving. The sky was rushing by above me. It would be dark and stormy with big black clouds flying by and rain coming hard and heavy, then suddenly the rain would stop and a large blue patch of sunny sky would open up with little cotton-ball clouds racing across the sky. Then long grey streamer-type clouds would fly through, followed by dark rain clouds and another blast of rain. It went like this all day on the road. I found it interesting that there was no thunder or lightning through the whole process—just powerful winds, rain and flying clouds.

I traveled 140 miles in seven hours through a mountain range. It was as exhilarating as anything I had ever experienced, and when I rolled into the town of Corner Brook, I didn't even feel tired. I thought this was quite an introduction to the "Rock".

I cycled to a gas station outside of Corner Brook just before sunset and asked the station attendant if he wouldn't mind me camping near the side of his building out of the wind. He looked at me and said, "Lord almighty, were you out in the wind today on a bike?" I responded, "Yes," and said that I had come from Port aux Basques. He shook his head in disbelief and said, "Sure, go ahead."

I was up early with a beautiful sunny day and a moderate tailwind on the road. I cycled along the very scenic and rugged Humber River into Deer Lake. After a short stop, I continued westward and had a vehicle pass me with a silver trailer unit attached. The driver began sounding his horn, started to brake and moved to the side of the road. As I came upon the vehicle, four people were on the side of the road clapping their hands. I recognized Jimmy and his family. What a nice surprise! Jimmy came running up and gave me a hug and said, "You have to tell me everything that happened." I said I surely would. Then I shook his parents' hands and said hello to the older daughter, who ignored me, as teenagers are apt to do.

Having a great day on the highway in Newfoundland

We agreed to meet at a camp spot about fifteen miles from where we were on the Trans-Canada highway. So they left and I pedaled the distance with a happy heart. Sure enough, by the time I got there, they had set up their campsite, had a fire going and Jimmy's dad had a glass of cold water waiting for me. So I camped with the family that night, about twenty miles east of Springdale.

We had a great supper prepared by Jimmy's mom and we talked far into the evening. Jimmy sat bedside me on one of the lawn chairs. He continually asked questions about my trip and especially wanted to know what I did during the hurricane. He asked me, "Where in Canada haven't you been?"

I replied that Canada was a very big place and it would take years to see it all by bicycle, but the key places I had not included in my trip were the Yukon, Northwest Territories, Labrador, Vancouver Island and PEI—the latter the short form for Prince Edward Island.

The family and I continued talking, and even the teenage daughter chipped in with a few questions as she listened. The fire was nice, and the evening was quiet and beautiful with a starlit sky. Everyone began yawning and I looked over at Jimmy, who was just managing to keep his eyes open. So we said goodnight and I crawled into my tent.

I awoke next morning to the smell of bacon, eggs and coffee. I went over to the washroom facility and cleaned up and walked back to the family. They were preparing breakfast and invited me to eat with them.

Jimmy deliberately sat by me. We finished breakfast and I helped them pack their gear since they were driving to St. John's that day. They then planned to take the ferry from Argentia back to the mainland. I shook hands and thanked them for their hospitality. They got into the car but Jimmy hesitated and then came over to me. He said, "I'm going to bicycle across Canada when I get older and I'm going to go to Yuk, Vancouber Island, PIE Island,

Labordor and the North Territories."

I said, "Great, Jimmy. You will be seeing a huge, beautiful country and that would be a special challenge for a young man like you to accomplish. You would be like a coureur de bois or a voyageur."

He had a look of curiosity on his face and I know he wanted to ask, "What's a coureur de bois and voyageur?" But his dad called so I knelt down and he hugged me and got into the car. He waved to me from his window as they drove away. I figured he would find out about the coureurs de bois and the voyageurs for himself. He was a smart kid.

I cycled 110 miles that day in hot weather and a crosswind and arrived at Terra Nova National Park. The cycling was long and lonely. Distance between places were measured in forty- to sixty-mile chunks with almost nothing in between, just miles of bush, rock, rivers, ponds and lakes.

I cycled through the town of Gander and stopped to buy insulin and supplies. I had treated my diabetes with a basic dose of thirty-five units of long-acting insulin per day. However, since the trip would end in another few days, I decided to get short-acting insulin (we used to call it "Toronto insulin" because it had been discovered by Banting and Best in Toronto) since my work load would drop off drastically once I stopped cycling. The less work, the more short-acting insulin I would need to compensate.

In the late afternoon, I came upon road crews and forest rangers working at extinguishing a forest fire. There was smoke everywhere and I could see fire breakouts in the forest, which the men would run to put out with heavy water canisters strapped to their backs. I immediately asked a ranger if they might need help, as I was ready to volunteer. He declined my offer. He said that the fire had been burning for two days and that they'd pretty much got it out by then. "Thanks for the offer, but you should have been here two days ago if you wanted to get into the firefighting business," he said, smiling. Damn, I would have loved to work at putting out a forest fire!

I continued for approximately another twenty miles when I came upon an incredible sight. From the crest of the next hill, two huge moose were staring right at me, about a hundred yards away. The bull towered above the road. He must have been ten feet high, with muscles standing out at his shoulders and hips and a large rack of antlers. The other was a female, smaller, with no antlers.

Their size was astounding. I had seen moose in Ontario on several occasions, but none of them matched the enormity of these Newfoundland behemoths. The bull was black-coated and his fur had a healthy, glossy sheen. I knew if the bull—a very powerful, aggressive and fast animal—were to get upset, he would cover the hundred-yard distance between us in the blink of an eye. Bull moose during mating season are known to charge trains head on, unfortunately to their certain demise. They fear nothing in the wild. So I didn't move and waited patiently.

Both the bull and female locked their eyes on me for a long time. They stood stock still for well over ten minutes, just watching. The female began chewing her cud after a while and swung her head over to the bull to nuzzle with it. He continued not to move. The female became more insistent and, finally, the bull lowered his massive head and nuzzled her on the neck with his snout. Then, as if nothing had happened at all, and with no backward glance, they slowly ambled off the road and disappeared into the bush. That was a hold-your-breath experience, but extremely grand. I was watching the uncontested king and queen of the wild royally walk by me without the slightest acknowledgement of my existence. How humbling!

I left Terra Nova National Park after breakfast and cycled into a moderate headwind with very hilly terrain. The ride was beautiful because the scenery was remarkable, with steep cliff rock faces, crashing streams, miles of greenery, and crystal-blue lakes scattered along the way. The highway must have been new, because it was very wide with six-foot-wide paved shoulders, and the tar pavement was deep black, as if it had been laid the day before. Further, it was as smooth as silk to bike on; I didn't feel one bump during my ride through the park.

I cycled ninety-five miles that day to Clarenville and stayed in an old empty barn along the highway. There was a pile of dry hay in the corner of the barn, which I formed into a mattress on which to put my sleeping bag.

Sleep came easy that evening, with a ceiling above to protect me from the elements and a soft homemade mattress below. As I drifted off, lines from the poem I'd learned from my Thunder Bay friend Bob O'Hara came back to me: "Been around Canada a bit/been from coast to coast … some nights I sleep in grand hotels/Most nights I sleep in barns …" Though I hadn't had any nights in a grand hotel, I could now truthfully say I'd been from coast to coast and slept in a barn.

I awoke to cold weather my last day on the road. I could see my breath—and a mild northerly wind and heavy ground fog. I said to myself, fog or no fog, I would make St. John's that day.

I was alone on the highway almost all day. Two cars passed me going west and one car passed going east. I struggled all day in the fog, trying to get to speed on my bike—I could have sworn I was hauling weight. I even stopped and oiled my chain and wheels, thinking that the oil might allow me to get going a little faster. I only learned later, when I arrived in St. John's, that for almost a hundred miles in the fog I had risen a half of a mile to the top of the Topsail Mountain Range. I saw nothing of the landscape or ocean around St. John's as everything was blotted out by fog except the road about fifteen feet in front of me.

I stopped at a gas station about four miles out of St. John's to take a break. I leaned my bike against the building and sat on the front step, realizing I was close to accomplishing my goal. I became very tired as I sat there and then I closed my eyes and went to sleep. I must have been out of it for about fifteen minutes when a man tapped me on the shoulder. He asked, "Are you tired?" For some reason I couldn't respond immediately. I tried to get up and my arms and legs wouldn't do what I wanted them to do. The man said, "Are you all right?"

I now knew what was going on and managed to say to him, "Sweet," and then, "Sugar." I tried to reach for my MedicAlert chain around my neck. Realizing what I was trying to do, he reached for the chain and pulled the medallion out and said, "Type 1 Diabetic. Oh my God, you're going into an insulin reaction." He called out to someone behind me and said, "Get me some apple juice from the cooler."

I said to myself, in slow motion, "That's ... right ... apple ... juice ... should ... do ... the ... trick."

That unfortunate event allowed me the pleasure of meeting Heber and Shirley Peach, owners of the gas station, who lived in Conception Bay. I stayed with these very nice people and their family for three days. I was shown around the area and picnicked beside several beautiful ponds (in Newfoundland, "ponds" are like small lakes). They also took me out in a large motor boat to go "jig" fishing for squid and cod.

"Jigging" is done with a hook and a silvery weight, which shines in the water when pulled up and down in a regular motion. This regular motion attracts the fish to bite. We filled the boat with squid and large cod. Then I got a big tug on my line and of course, being the fishing neophyte, I thought it was another cod, which I had caught before. But this fish was sluggish, not really fighting hard, and was very heavy to pull up from the depths. I said to the men in the boat, "I think I've got a big cod on the line," so they watched as I dragged it in hand over hand. I kept looking into the dark water trying to make out how big it was. Suddenly, I saw this huge dark form coming towards me. It looked like the bottom of the ocean was coming up with this thing. I almost dropped the line when I saw two eyes on the same side of this fish's head stare up at me. I screamed and then yelled, "It's a mutant!" The guy beside me grabbed the line and pulled a huge flat fish (halibut) into the boat.

Then they laughed till they cried and one fellow had to take a pee over the side of the boat, as they couldn't contain their hilarity. I was called the crazy "mainlander" over that event. Even when I was about to go to St. John's, they were trying to act serious about my leaving until somebody said, "Watch out for the 'mutants,'" which resulted in gales of laughter and one guy falling into an armchair since he was laughing so hard he couldn't catch his breath and could no longer stand up. Needless to say, I had three great days at the Peach family residence.

The end of the road – Vancouver to St. John's, 4,785 miles!

I cycled to the city sign for St. John's and got my picture taken by a gentleman walking on the roadside. I lifted my bike over my head in triumph. I continued into the city of St. John's, the oldest English-founded settlement in North America. Tradition has it that the city got its name when explorer John Cabot became the first European to sail into the harbor, on June 24, 1497, the feast day of Saint John the Baptist. Then I sought out the city hall to get an

157

official document confirming the completion of my bike trip across Canada. I brought diary notes and newspaper clippings to prove my claims to the administration.

It turned out the Peach family had already called Mayor Dorothy Wyatt and advised her to expect me. I went to the reception desk and told the lady what I wanted. She said, "One minute, please," and called Dorothy saying, "The young man you've been waiting for is here." She hung up and said, "The mayor will see you now." Wow! What hospitality and service!

So I got to talk to the mayor for about a half hour about the trip and what I was planning to do with my life. I was then given a special invitation to attend the Regatta at Quidi Vidi, (pronunciations vary, even among longtime residents, but "Kiddy Viddy" is the most common), a small lake on the edge of the city. I attended the Royal St. John's Regatta, which is held the first Wednesday in August, and had a very good time with people congratulating me and wanting to shake my hand. I left the regatta in the late afternoon and went to the "End of the World" hostel.

The next day, I traveled around the city doing some sightseeing. Anyone in Newfoundland will tell you that one of the most recognizable landmarks in the province is Signal Hill, or more specifically, Cabot Tower. Cabot Tower was built in 1897 to commemorate the four-hundredth anniversary of John Cabot's discovery of Newfoundland and Queen Victoria's Diamond Jubilee. Marconi received the first trans-Atlantic wireless message at a position near the tower—the letter "S" in Morse code sent from Cornwall, England, in 1901.

I discovered that Cabot Tower is the centre of the Signal Hill National Historic Park, Canada's second largest historic park, with walking trails and an interpretation centre where the visitor can hear very interesting stories about the area. Hikers will see spectacular views of the city, the harbor and the ocean. I also watched the military perform in the Signal Hill Tattoo, a re-enactment of military exercises from the eighteenth century complete with period costumes, guns and cannon fire.

I then traveled out of town by hitchhiking and went to Cape Spear, the most easterly point of land in North America; the next landfall is either Ireland or England, across the Atlantic. The oldest surviving lighthouse in Newfoundland is located there and has been restored to its 1839 appearance. The visitor center contains exhibits on the history of lighthouses and the tradition of lighthouse-keeping. The site is surrounded by spectacular scenery and wildlife. I saw a huge pod of whales, large seabirds and icebergs within a short distance of the rocky coastline. The whales were swimming and diving about four hundred yards off Cape Spear and making wondrous sounds while blowing water and air out of their blowholes.

Next day, I had to re-adjust my insulin dose to accommodate for my sitting around. I included regular short-acting insulin to my long-acting insulin base. I took the train out of St. John's back to Port aux Basques to catch the ferry to North Sydney. I learned later that Glen arrived four days after I did in St. John's and had successfully completed the trip as well.

I felt, in a very small part, that I had experienced something of what the voyageur tradition was about. The terrain, the elements and the raw power of nature were unrelenting and a challenge for any adventurer willing to leave civilization somewhat behind.

Of course, my experience was limited to a small narrow patch of black pavement stretching across Canada, with all the comforts of home within my reach if I wanted them. I was never truly alone or without help as the voyageurs or coureurs de bois were during their early adventures in Canada. They were tough, smart and determined to do the things they did in opening up Canada. I'm afraid I learned that I would be no match for them.

STATISTICS
Vancouver, British Columbia, to St. John's,
Newfoundland
June 6 to August 1

Total Miles Traveled	4,785
Total Days	56
Total Biking Days	49
Average Miles per Day	98
Most Miles per Day	145
Fewest Miles per Day	40

But I did learn other things from my experience. I learned that Canada, through the small window from which I saw her, is a beautiful, vast country; that human beings in the most part are giving and generous and love to hear a good story; that diabetes will not stop me from doing anything I set my mind to do; that partnerships can be dissolved by factors that are completely out of your control; and that a little child can carry the torch of future dreams higher and brighter than your own.

Cape Spear – next stop Ireland

DON'T YOU JUST LOVE IT WHEN THIS HAPPENS?

1. You're rushing between flights and realize you have to take your insulin. You look for the closest washroom and run towards it. Once inside you go to the far end of the row of sinks, place your insulin bag on the counter and take out your blood sugar meter, needles and insulin vial. You complete your blood test and take your needle and vial and begin the process of drawing up. In walks airport security and asks you, "What the hell are you doing?"

2. You're making a special presentation to a large audience. As you're waiting for your cue, you begin sweating from your forehead and temples. Your hands start shaking and you feel the need to sit down. Soon you are in a full-blown insulin reaction, when a friend comes by to wish you luck and recognizes immediately what's wrong. As he helps you out, you continue to sweat on your forehead, your back and your legs. By the time you have to make your presentation, you are a sopping wet mess in a suit jacket but still you go on and make the presentation, hoping no one notices.

3. Have you ever taken an injection of insulin and then pulled the syringe out, only to find the syringe has come away but the needle is still embedded in your skin?

4. Have you ever taken an injection and found the plunger won't move because something has plugged the neck of the syringe and will not allow you to administer the dose, so you have to start over and inject a second time?

5. Have you ever had a grandma who would continue to ask you if you wanted more food at a Christmas dinner even though she knows you are a diabetic? (Of course, this is done out of love and not quite understanding what diabetes really is.) Then, after you've eaten a full meal, she rushes over to you and says she has an assortment of goodies for desert: strawberry, cherry, apple, pecan pies and chocolate cake. She happily suggests that she can give you very small pieces of all of them because she knows you can't eat a lot of sweets.

6. You're at a sales meeting and are making a presentation. Lunch arrives and you leave to go someplace private to take your insulin before eating. You decide to inject your stomach. Returning to the boardroom you line up for lunch when someone close to you says, "Are you bleeding?" You are surprised by the question so you ask, "What do you mean?" She points to the middle of your white shirt and there's a large blotch of dark red blood on it from the injection you have just taken.

7. Isn't it great to take your insulin injection and get it over with? But sometime afterward, you forget and you doubt whether you have taken it. Your blood sugar meter is at home. You start asking yourself, "Did I or didn't I?" It bothers you all afternoon but you don't want to inject again for fear of hypoglycemia, but you should inject again in case of hyperglycemia.

8. It's your last bottle of insulin and you're telling yourself you've got to get to the pharmacy to buy some more vials before this one runs out. So you're reaching to grab the vial when your best buddy, Dude the cat, jumps up on the dresser to say hello and bumps the vial onto the tile floor. It shatters into a million shards. You stand stock-still because you have no slippers on while you wait for someone to rescue you.

9. It's late and you're walking along the beach near the Pacific Ocean at Stanley Park, in Vancouver. It's a beautiful warm evening with a full moon and stars everywhere. You lie down on the beach using a log as a pillow as you watch the heavens. You are awakened by a firm tap on the shoulder. You notice you're wet from sweat and starting to shiver. You clumsily get up. The RCMP officer asks, "Have you been drinking?" You respond slowly, "No I haven't." He asks you to come over to the car. He patiently waits as you slowly follow him. He uses the breathalyzer and you blow zero. Next, he checks your eyes and the pupils are dilated, so he asks if you have taken drugs. "No," you slowly respond. He sighs impatiently and says, "How about medication?" "Yes," you slowly respond. He says, "What kind?" "Insulin," you reply. "Oh jeez," he exclaims in a panic, "not another diabetic!"

10. You've gone into an insulin reaction just before supper but manage to make it to the table and proceed to eat everything that's on your plate. As you come out of the reaction, your mom asks you, "How was dinner?" and you answer, "I don't know! What did we have?"

Tale # 8
STEEL LEGS AND KIDNEY TRANSPLANT

Late in mid-life, I experienced many of the long-term
complications from diabetes, which I have outlined in this
story. However, I decided that my physical challenges
would not stop me in my fight against diabetes.

As a Type 1 diabetic, I have led a very healthy,
active and varied life, as the things I've done will bear out:
bicycling across Canada and Europe; kayaking the old
voyageur route from Banff, Alberta, to Winnipeg,
Manitoba; running a few twenty-mile charity marathons;
participating in football, track, other sporting activities;
graduating from university; and working for the U.N., in
Rome. Most of my life, I've been told about the long-term
complications from diabetes. I was diagnosed at two years
of age and lived the first thirty-one years of my life with
diabetes with little or no control. This was neither my fault
nor that of the health-care professionals who were
responsible for my care.

I lived my early years in a techno/knowledge limbo
concerning diabetes, in which the protocol for diabetes was
diet, one injection of insulin (Toronto and lente beef/pork)
and urine testing to monitor blood sugar control. Needles
(27 steel gauge), in my early childhood, were sharpened on
a flint stone by my dad, and the needle and syringe were
boiled by my mom in a pot of water before each injection.
They were used over and over again. Further, urine testing

was performed by placing an inch of blue Benedict's solution in a test tube with ten drops of urine and boiling the mixture in a pot of water. The solution would change to different colors and these colors were assumed to represent my blood sugar.

The accuracy of the color of the urine test was highly tenuous vis-à-vis what was actually happening in my bloodstream. For example, I remember as a small boy feeling extremely weak and shaky for my urine test to finish. The final test color was orange, which supposedly indicated high blood sugar. I turned from the stove to inform my mom and fell heavily because my blood sugar was actually low. So much for accuracy in urine testing, and yet these crude tests were the be-all and end-all of diabetic control in those days! Sterile packaged needles arrived when I was approximately nine years old. They were quite a marvelous invention and also were very sharp, which saved me some pain.

The old protocols would be laughed at today by health-care professionals, or by diabetic patients who have learned current control techniques using blood monitoring devices and multiple injections or insulin pumps. The new concepts and devices were provided to me in my thirty-first year, when I developed retinal detachment in my left eye.

The surgery for my blind left eye was performed in Memphis, Tennessee, by Dr. Steve Charles, an American doctor who pioneered retinal attachment surgery (vitrectomy). It cost over $16,000. My surgery was successful and the following care from my doctors in Calgary (Dr. M. Kirker and Dr. S. Ross) was also exceptional. My diabetic life changed from one injection a day to four insulin injections per day and monitoring by blood sugar measurement. My daily blood sugar became fairly good and my repaired eyes have lasted to the time of my writing this book at fifty-seven years.

I inform you of these things because I believe, if I had had better control during my early developing years and into adulthood, I might not have experienced the story I am about to outline for you, which occurred in my later years. Notice I said, "Might not have experienced." Type 1 diabetes is a lifelong affliction, which affects your body twenty-four hours a day, every day of your life. There is no mercy or reprieve. The disease is like a slow rot in your body that robs you over time of the organs that provide you with a quality life. Insulin gives you time to live but does not rid you of the demon that destroys your inner body slowly and persistently as you age. Good control may stem the tide but it can't overcome the disease. Only a cure can.

My first experience, after my eye surgery, with my accelerating poor health occurred when I was thirty-nine. I was playing basketball with friends when my right leg cramped up and a searing pain shot through my leg. I had to quit the game and later set up an appointment to have my leg looked at. The doctors found my pulse to be very feeble in my leg, and I had areas in both my feet that didn't show pain or feeling when poked with a steel pin. I was also informed that my kidneys were not in normal range for creatinine levels in my bloodstream. All these problems were attributed to long years of diabetes. My heart was also tested but everything seemed fine with that organ.

My initial reaction was to start training to strengthen my legs, and I set a goal for myself that I would run ten kilometers on my fortieth birthday. The running and training hurt but I knew of no other way to get good blood flow back into my blood-starved legs. After about two months of steady running with pain, the pain disappeared one day. I then increased my run distances until I was doing at least one ten-kilometer run per week and weight training for my upper body. On my fortieth birthday I ran the ten kilometers with my consulting doctor and good friend Don and finished with no pain and felt very good about my accomplishment.

My kidney creatinine measures, however, continued to rise and my doctors kept close watch on me. I continued to run occasionally and do some weight training, but nowhere near the level that I had done for my fortieth birthday. In my forty-eighth year, my doctor warned me that my creatinine levels were getting around the 400 range (normal is 80 to 120) and that I would automatically become a dialysis patient when the number passed the 600 mark. I was given some medications and a special diet, but unlike with my legs, I myself could do nothing for this failing organ.

Then, when I was forty-nine, my right leg developed a nagging and continuous pain twenty-four hours a day that over-the-counter pain medications could not eliminate (diabetic ischemic leg disease). A small black patch appeared on the side of my big toe, indicating gangrene. Review with a vascular specialist confirmed what I had already observed: my blood vessels were blocked in my leg.

My leg muscles were in a continuous state of cramping and pain, demanding that my body provide more blood for them to function. I was prescribed a powerful narcotic to ease the pain and allow me to sleep at night. To try to obtain more relief throughout the night, the doctor also advised me to hang my right leg over the bedside to allow gravity to drain blood down into my aching leg. I asked him, "How long will this last?" I assumed it would end at some time. He looked at me for a long minute and bowed his head and said quietly, "It will last as long as you can take the pain. And then we amputate."

I didn't ask any more questions but I went home in shock. In my head I kept hearing him saying something about amputation but surely he couldn't mean me. Just tell me what to do and I'll do it: drugs, electric stimulation, physiotherapy, surgery: anything, but don't tell me I'll lose my leg. How would I care for my family and myself with no leg? I would be useless! I felt desperate and alone. I started to cry. Then my mood changed to anger and I yelled out that there was no way they were going to take my leg without a fight.

After informing my wife and my kids about what was happening and having a very emotional family meeting, I began my search for answers. I reviewed newspapers, health magazines, library books, scientific and medical reviews and the Internet. It took about six weeks of searching until I came upon a small reference in a newspaper indicating that St. Elizabeth's Hospital in Boston was testing a procedure on diabetics with ischemic leg disease.

They seemed to have had some success. I got onto the Internet and pulled all the information I could. Their first test of recombinant DNA VegF (vascular endothelial growth factor) had proven relatively successful on five patients with vascular leg pain. The hospital was seeking volunteers to continue testing the new medication. My choice was easy: stay at home till they cut my leg off or take a risk with VegF in Boston.

After a discussion with my doctor, who approved of my filling in the appropriate forms and attempting the procedure, I went to Boston—the only Canadian to do so. I had to go through several tests to prove that I was an appropriate candidate for the treatment. Those expensive tests had to be paid for by me, as neither my insurance firm nor the Ontario or federal governments were going to invest money in a new, untried research medication. So preliminary testing (CT scan, MRI, blood tests, x-rays, eye testing, electrical stimulation tests, pain sensitivity tests, physical exam, brain scan, etc.), air flights to Boston, accommodation, food and taxis were paid by me to the tune of $30,000.

Once I passed the testing process, all medical expenses were then covered under the research grant at St. Elizabeth's. I went through the research process for three months with usually two visits per week to Boston for checkups. The Boston doctor (Dr. Jeffrey Isner, now deceased) informed me that my blood tests were showing that my creatinine levels were high and that I should see my kidney doctor back in Canada. I agreed.

I received VegF through eight intramuscular injections into my calf muscle. I found the procedure painful, not from the injections, but from the volume of VegF they put into the muscle. My leg was sore for hours afterwards. However, that was a small price to pay in hopes of saving my leg. The research papers I read indicated that VegF would achieve its objective three weeks from time of injection. The medication's goal was to generate new vascularization (blood vessels) in the leg, specifically in the muscles exhibiting pain symptoms. It was as if the muscles were calling out for something to help them and VegF was answering their painful call.

CAT scans after the fact showed pictures of my leg with cascading, new small blood vessels throughout the region of leg pain. As predicted, the pain I had been experiencing for eight months disappeared three weeks after the injections. My leg was fully functional and actually was stronger than my untreated leg.

I thanked my lucky stars for my due diligence and determination in finding an answer to the crisis. I could run, weight train, and walk in the malls or in the park again. It was a tremendous feeling of accomplishment and satisfaction. But my happiness would be short-lived, as my personal enemy, diabetes, was doing its worst to spoil things for me.

Four months after the success with my right leg, my blood test came back and the doctor was reviewing it. My wife, Maria, and I sat down in the chairs in his office to wait. I was fifty-one years old; it was January and he turned to me and in a low voice said, "Your creatinine levels are at 625." My wife and I looked at each other; we both knew what that meant. My wife began to cry and I asked again if there was anything I could do to stay off dialysis.

He said, "No. Your body is filling with toxins and poisons as we speak and is taking on more water and not getting rid of it. That is why your face, joints and feet are swelling. We will start immediately."

"Hold it," I said angrily. "What happens if I don't want to do this?"

The doctor said, "You can go home and die. It will

take a while but your body will not take the abuse both from your kidneys and your diabetic condition for very long."

He waited for me to respond. The answer was obvious: go for dialysis.

I was very angry and became depressed. Further, my left leg started paining me as my right leg had done three years before. I experienced constant pain and had to take narcotics and hang my leg over the side of the bed one more time. Finally, gangrene set in my toes. I applied to St. Elizabeth's Hospital a second time but the response was that since I had developed kidney failure, I no longer fit the research protocol. I then wrote the FDA and several other U.S. universities and hospitals where similar research was ongoing: no success. Realizing that no help was in sight to stop the pain, I made the decision to amputate my left leg below the knee (BKA). This happened in May, after I had been on hemodialysis for five months.

The narcotics for pain had a strange effect on me. I hallucinated and became delusional. I found my hallucinations were happy experiences and grand adventures. I dreamed of visions so real I couldn't distinguish my dream world from reality. I had visions of cute baby animals around my bed. Kittens, bunny rabbits, puppy dogs and fawns visited with me every day and showed great affection. I would leave my room on my flying mattress, which would take me to the Rockies, over the western prairies and all manner of places in Canada. The delusions seemed so genuine that I felt the heat from the sun, wind in my face, cold from the glaciers in the mountains, and dampness when it rained on me. And the colors were magnificent.

I was totally involved in my own world of make-believe. Maria became concerned about my mental state and called a meeting with my doctor and a pharmacist to review what was happening.

"How are you doing?" the doctor asked.

"Things are going fine," I said.

171

Then he asked a number of factual questions, which I answered correctly. My demeanor appeared normal and the doctor didn't see a problem. He turned to the pharmacist to say something when I told him not to move because he would scare the aliens standing behind him. Startled, he looked behind him and said, "What aliens?"

And I said, "The ones standing behind you." I must have been very convincing because my drug regimen was immediately reviewed and changes were made, which provided much better results in relation to my mental health and my view of reality.

But now my mood was foul and aggressive. I was deeply depressed about my situation and took it out on anybody in sight. The dialysis process did not help, as I would often get sick on the blood-cleaning machine and retch. I never felt well on dialysis and lost a lot of weight. My water intake had to be limited and I wasn't allowed certain foods such as oranges.

The sheer boredom of sitting in an uncomfortable chair, frequently getting the chills, shivering and asking for a blanket or two, was par for the course. Sometimes blacking out or vomiting all over myself was my lot for four to five hours per day, three days a week, and this would go on until I died or was able to get a kidney transplant. The queue for a transplanted kidney was approximately four thousand patients long, with a waiting time of five to seven years.

The atmosphere within the dialysis unit was depressingly silent and hopeless, interrupted only by the sound of someone getting sick, crying or vocally expressing anger. Most of the patients were in their fifties or older. About sixty percent of them were there because of diabetes. One of the younger patients I met was a twenty-seven year old diabetic, blind and on hemodialysis. He would not respond when he was asked questions. Another diabetic patient, a happy alcoholic, would come in for dialysis when he decided to. Although he was phoned by staff to remind him and received all kinds of warnings of what might happen if he failed to come in, he continued with his defiance and crazy belief that he would not die from kidney failure. He died shortly after my arrival one day by staggering into a speeding car as he walked home on the highway.

The nurses and doctors were heroes in a losing war. Few of these patients would be candidates for a kidney transplant. Those few who were potential candidates would probably die in their chairs waiting for an appropriate donor or develop complications over time that would disqualify their candidacy. Being on dialysis was a ridiculous extension of a no-win situation rather than a hope of a future.

My kidney doctor asked me several times to speak to an in-house psychiatrist to discuss my depression and anger. I told him forcefully that I was in no mood to speak to anyone except the person who would get me out of this personal hell. So I continued in my depressed state for two months. One day, a new person came into the unit. He had on the typical white lab coat of hospital staff and was walking around speaking to different patients. He was soon guided into the nurse's office and stayed there for approximately twenty minutes. When he came out, he was no longer wearing his white coat and he came directly over to my chair. He sat down beside me and I deliberately ignored him. He sat there for at least fifteen minutes without speaking. Finally, I said angrily, "What the hell are you hanging around me for?"

He said, "I hear you need a friend."

"A friend?" I said. "I don't even know who the hell you are!" And, I continued in a loud voice, "You can tell those nurses to stop talking about me behind my back. Then I said, "Now take off and bother someone else."

He laughed and said, "But I have no one else to bother and I have at least forty-five minutes left before I leave the unit."

That irked me even more. Didn't this dummy get the message? Another ten minutes of silence and he was still there. Finally I said, "Look, buddy, what do you want?"

He softly said, "What's bothering you?"

I looked at him and shouted, "What's bothering me! Are you crazy? Isn't it obvious?"

He smiled and said, "No, it's not."

Well, that was it! I would tell this idiot in no uncertain terms what was wrong and even a moron like this should get my meaning. So after almost an hour of detailing in a very direct manner (with expletives) everything that had happened to get me to this rotten place, I finally shut up and took a breath.

He looked at me and said, "Well, that's quite a story. I want to take the time to think about the things you said and see you again in a couple of days after we take a few blood tests. Is that okay with you?"

Strangely enough, I said, "Yes." Somehow, I also felt better. Actually, I was sorry to see him go.

My mood changed after that outburst with the stranger. I wondered if he would really come back. I kept quiet and did not hassle anybody during my next couple of dialysis sessions. I also started to become more aware of the workings of the unit: the characteristics of the nurses, the way they handled difficult situations, whether they were jokers or serious in their attitudes toward working with patients. I gained a volume of knowledge about these people and the patients they treated by watching them instead of bemoaning my plight.

Soon the stranger came back, this time in a white coat. He said, "How are you doing?"

I said, "I'm doing better."

He said he knew that from the good report he received from the nurses. "They have noticed a change in your behavior, but you are still too quiet."

I told him I thought I'd better keep my mouth shut for a while because it was always getting me into trouble. He laughed. He finally introduced himself as the in-hospital psychiatrist. He wanted me to take anti-depressants for a while because my serotonin levels were low. I agreed. We talked a bit more and then he left.

Over the next two to three weeks, I became a different person. I started looking up jokes on the Internet and memorizing them to tell nurses and patients. To fill the silence of the unit, I would sing songs at the top of my lungs and soon had patients singing along with me. I became a prankster, pulling tricks on patients and nurses alike. I would fake being sick so I would have nurses run over to check me out and then tickle them when they least expected it.

Dialysis became fun because I found that most of the staff and patients wanted an excuse to laugh or sing. I became an entertainer. Soon I had patients coming in early to make sure they got a seat near me. Nurses would tell me that they were disappointed because they were not selected to be in my section during their shift. However, my antics were not appreciated by all patients and nurses, and I made sure I didn't cross the line with these people.

In my eighteen months with dialysis, I was aware of several deaths in the unit. I'm sure there were others but we as patients were not told why someone had left. Usually it was another dialysis patient who was a friend of the deceased who would let us know. Nurses would look the other way and become busy with something when someone would ask what had happened to so-and-so. In a small group of sick people, these events were chilling and demoralizing.

A good dialysis friend of mine, who would join me in my funny antics, had been on dialysis for six years. He was fifty-four years old; he could not get a kidney transplant because of the disease he had. He seemed as healthy as you can be on dialysis. He was generally in good spirits and one weekend told me he was going to work on his roof. He finished the repairs on his roof and then died of a heart attack. The dialysis machines work the heart really hard in draining the blood out of your body for cleansing. Many of the patients' deaths were from heart failure,

175

infectious complications, old age and suicide. Being tied to a machine for survival has a way of wearing the human body and spirit out quickly!

I had been in the dialysis unit for over a year now. Things were passable there. I kept up the jokes, tricks and singing because I couldn't stand the gloomy silence that pervaded the place. It was sometime in February that I started to experience minor pain in my right, VegF-treated leg. Then I reported to my doctor that I had a black patch forming on my middle toe. I had already guessed what had happened before the doctor informed me. My VegF leg had lasted four years but diabetes, my constant companion, had ruined a good thing again.

At the same time, my wife got tested to have one of her two kidneys transplanted into me. After almost two months of tests, Maria was informed she could not be my donor. She was very upset. My brother Bob then volunteered to give me one of his kidneys. After months of testing, my brother was accepted in early May as a potential donor for me. Once we had a donor established, I was put through a number of physical tests and psychological and social interviews to check me out. In other words, was I a normal person with good common sense and a clear understanding of what I was getting into?

I found out during this testing process that donors, unknown to them, may sometimes have only one functioning kidney and, in fact, cannot donate. Their single kidney does just fine for them. Many are surprised to learn this fact after testing. Sometimes the second kidney is deformed, is not connected to an artery, is very small or just does not work.

Of course, I didn't pass the physical test, as my leg had progressed to a state of extreme pain and the gangrene had grown on my toes. The doctor examining me said we would have to correct the situation in my leg before we could proceed with a kidney transplant. They were talking about re-routing blood vessels to get more blood into my leg.

I informed them that I wasn't going to go through a number of leg surgeries over at least a year for limited or no success. I had met other diabetic patients who had attempted these corrective surgeries, and they had gone through hell with no success. I informed them that my decision would be BKA of my second leg and the quicker the better. Within a week, I had my second leg amputation. The healing process was greatly accelerated by using the hyperbaric oxygen chamber. My stump healed completely in four weeks and my scheduled date for my kidney transplant surgery was August 24.

The staff and patients at the dialysis unit were very happy for me. For the patients, it was a dream they all wanted—to be freed from the dialysis chair and live a full life again. For the staff, they rejoiced in the brief and brilliant light of success when they were able to help at least one patient among the many desperate sufferers they attend to day after day.

I had patients shaking my hand and saying that I gave them all hope. Others cried and wished me well. Some were upset that I was leaving because no one would be around to joke and make them laugh. I told them they could do it themselves if they really wanted it. They didn't need me. They made me promise to come back and visit when I had healed from my kidney transplant and I said I would.

Things happened quickly. By the next day, I was on my way to the hospital with my brother. We were placed in separate rooms, had our IV fluids started and waited for our surgery time. My brother would go first to have his healthy kidney removed, and I would arrive later to have the kidney implanted in my lower left abdomen and attached to the iliac artery.

My two failed kidneys would stay but I would now carry a third healthy kidney in my body. As I was wheeled into the surgical theatre, which was cold, I began shivering; I saw my brother's kidney resting in solution by the surgical table. I asked the doctor how my brother's surgery had gone and he said it had gone very well and there were no concerns. I felt good about that.

As the surgical team moved around me, I waited for the anesthetic to be administered. A man, his face hidden behind a blue mask, asked, "How are you doing?"

I said, "Fine."

He said, "You might feel a slight stinging sensation in your arm. This is normal." A short time later he asked, "Do you feel it?" and I said, "Yes." "Now count slowly backwards from ten," he said. I think I got to six and I was out.

My next awareness was waking in the step-down unit and realizing I had something deep in my throat and chest. I tried to take a breath and I couldn't breathe. I reached up to pull it out but a hand was blocking my attempt. Then I started to struggle because I couldn't get air into me. Suddenly someone dressed in blue put something in the pipe that was in my mouth, and I dozed off again. Before doing so, I saw my youngest brother Mike, an anesthesiologist practicing in Calgary, standing by my bedside.

I went through this process several times in twelve hours. Each time, I couldn't breathe and each time I was knocked out. However, each time I awakened, I was able to pick up bits of information about what was going on. It seemed something had happened during surgery and I had water in my lungs. In my next wake up, I heard someone say, "Just a little bit longer" as I struggled to get the pipe out of my throat. I promised myself, before going under again, that I would force myself not to struggle and concentrate everything on trying to breathe.

Sure enough, my message to myself was effective. I became conscious again and I tried not to choke; I forcefully blew air out of my lungs and drew air in as hard as I could. The doctor leaning over me said "Good job," and I put a hand up and touched her face. She laughed. With that she made a decision to take the tube out of my throat and lungs. However, I was not yet home-free though I rejoiced at the relief that came when the first pipe was removed. Then another, shorter pipe was placed in my throat that made me gag. I was held there till I got used to it and the doctor said, "Good man." I was not knocked out again.

As I looked around, I saw Mike holding my hand and Maria crying and holding my other hand. My brother said, "Take it easy. You've just been through a lot." Of course, I wanted to ask him what had happened but I couldn't because the blasted pipe was in my mouth. I still felt no pain from the surgery, and I thought maybe I was having this difficulty breathing because the surgery had failed in some way. That scared me. Finally, the tube was removed from my throat and I spoke to the lady doctor who had stayed with me for twelve hours to assure my safe return to the world.

I was informed that the kidney surgery was successful but complications had set in from the moment I was anesthetized. They had attempted, at the beginning of surgery, to get a breathing tube down my throat. But my jaw and throat locked up and they couldn't get it in. Several members of the team attempted to get it in without success. So a senior anesthesiologist was called to perform the procedure.

He was successful, but the interruption took over an hour and my fresh kidney was not so fresh. Further, the drug Lasix (a diuretic) that they put into me at the start of surgery caused water to build up in my lungs over time. Therefore, when the surgery was complete, the only way they could dry my soggy lungs was to keep a pipe in my lungs so that the water would evaporate and then be breathed out. What a way to start a new life adventure!

After another few hours, I was moved to my room and put under intensive care. There were IVs everywhere and I looked as if I was in a plastic cocoon of tubing that surrounded my bed. I also had a plastic collection bag with a catheter inserted in my penis (happily this was done during surgery when I was unconscious) to collect any urine my new kidney generated so that it could be measured accurately.

The problem was that my new kidney was not generating much urine. This was blamed on the length of time the kidney was left outside my body, the shock factor of surgery and the amount of Lasix that was administered during surgery. All these factors were making my body swell with the collection of excess liquid, which could not be eliminated by my new kidney. We just had to wait. Finally, the dam broke and volumes of urine came out of my body as my new kidney became functional. The swelling began to disappear.

I still had a reminder of my days on dialysis: the catheter that had been surgically placed in my chest as my attachment to the dialysis machine was still there, hanging from my chest. However, I was informed that a doctor would be coming to free me from this constant nuisance. Soon the doctor arrived at my bedside, injected the local anesthetic around the site in my chest, cut me and removed the piping that had been in my body for eighteen months. As I saw the last of the pipe coming out, I yelled, "Free! Thank God almighty! Free at last!" I startled the poor doctor so badly that he dropped the piping on the floor. I started to laugh and once he realized what was going on, he laughed also.

My remaining days in the hospital were uneventful, as I healed quickly and felt much better with my new kidney doing its job. Soon I was on my way home, where I relaxed for a couple of weeks before starting my next big commitment. I had to learn to walk on two amputated legs.

My rehabilitation would take place at St. John's Rehab Hospital and I would be closely monitored by a very friendly, professional and precise young woman called Shirlene, who wouldn't take "I can't do it" from any patient. She immediately began my exercises, especially on my lower back, thighs and core area. I didn't realize there were so many ways to torture someone. I discovered muscles that I never knew I had and they hurt. There was always a big smile from her while I suffered and a "Surely you can do more than that!" or "Come on. Just one more!" Good God! When would it end?

Finally after weeks of exercises, I was allowed to get my prosthetic legs on and attempt to walk. My prosthetic legs were made by an old University of Waterloo classmate of mine up in Barrie, north of Toronto. We hadn't been in contact for almost twenty-five years, but when I needed prosthetics made, his business was one of the few that were mentioned, although I still didn't realize Jim was the owner.

So I decided to go to Barrie and see what they offered. I entered his place of business, Prosthetics /Orthotics Barrie, in my wheelchair and spoke to the receptionist, explaining what I wanted. She said Jim would be out in a moment. As soon as I saw him, I knew who he was. Jim had been a competitive swimmer at U of Wat. and had been an excellent student. It was good seeing someone from my past, and the prospect of getting prosthetic legs from someone I knew bolstered my confidence.

I learned that my legs would be fitted in three phases. Phase 1 was fitted with the realization that my legs were still healing from the amputation. They were still swollen and therefore the first "legs" were made to provide room. I would compensate for the space by wearing socks over the stump. As the stumps became less swollen, more socks were added, until a second leg (phase 2) would be fitted, which more closely followed the shape of the reduced stumps.

Again, adjustments would be made with the addition or subtraction of socks covering the stumps. Finally, phase 3 was the final product. It takes approximately sixteen to twenty-four months to get to Phase 3 while the stumps completely heal. Even at Phase 3, the stumps can swell for any number of reasons. Sometimes you might not get the prosthetics on at all, or they can be very hard to get on and will cause you pain when you try to walk on them—sort of like a new pair of shoes and your aching feet.

So my first walking attempts with Shirlene, and for the remainder of my stay at St. John's Rehab, were made on my Phase 1 legs. I called them my "steel legs," much better sounding than "prosthetic legs," I thought. Jim said they should be called "titanium legs" because that was what they were really made of. My walking experience started by using parallel bars to hold onto as I walked the distance between the bars. I then graduated to using two canes and walking with supervision down the hallway, then using just one cane and increasing my walk distance in the hallways.

I also continued with my exercise regimen and was learning to "shuffle step," walk sideways, walk backwards, and walk with my head up and my back straight. Shirlene was very particular about these things and I was glad she was. I also had to play catch and play badminton to learn how to adjust quickly and keep my balance. I learned how to walk up stairs and move in a circular manner. Soon I moved up to walking on the treadmill and doing some weight training on my upper body. By this time, I was doing quite well and was waiting impatiently for Shirlene to let me leave the Rehabilitation Unit; I had been there for almost four months by then.

One day Shirlene asked, "What are you going to do with yourself when you go home?"

"Hell, I thought to myself, "I'm going to relax because I sure haven't had much rest here!" But I answered, "I don't know. I haven't really put that much thought into it."

She smiled and said, "When you come back for your next session, I want to hear you tell me some goals you have set for yourself."

You know, I was totally stumped. What was I going to do with two amputated legs, a transplanted kidney, limited vision and diabetes? The usual things started to come to mind: read books, play cards, walk around the block, visit friends, write to my friends on my computer, take care of the house, weed the garden, etc. In my mind all these things seemed pretty mundane. They were not goals

182

that I could really sink my teeth into, or a challenge.

Still not satisfied with what I had come up with, I turned to reading the evening paper. Reading through the articles, I came upon an announcement that the Juvenile Diabetes Research Foundation (JDRF) was organizing a walkathon in Toronto for diabetes research. I knew immediately what I was going to attempt to do. I would walk and raise money in the walkathon.

The next day, I called the JDRF and asked if a double amputee had ever walked in their walkathon. The lady was a bit startled by the question but said she would get the appropriate person for me to speak to. Marla came on the phone, and I asked my question again. She said she wasn't aware of any double amputees walking in their national or Toronto walkathon campaign, and she wasn't aware of any other charities doing walkathons that had double amputees walking. Single amputees, yes; double amputees, no. She then said, "Excuse me for asking, but are you a double amputee?"

"Yes," I replied, "and a Type 1 diabetic and a kidney transplant recipient."

Her comment then was, "Do you think you can walk five kilometers?"

I said, "Not now, but I could train myself to do it over the following months."

She said, "There would be no reason you couldn't participate in the walk as long as you had someone to supervise your progress."

I said, "Great, see you in May." And that is how I got involved in the "STEEL LEGS WALK" for JDRF research. When I arrived back at rehabilitation, I had some great stuff to tell Shirlene.

She said, "A very ambitious goal! With the remaining time here we'll work you harder on the treadmill to get you in better shape for the big event."

STEEL LEGS WALK
Team for the Juvenile Diabetes Research Foundation
(JDRF)
(top from left)
Dan Beriault, Dr. Mike & Sylvia Beriault, Dr. Don DuVall,
Nick Beriault, Hazel & Robert Bruce
(bottom from left)
Hercules Faga, Maria Beriault, Mig Migirdycan, Steve
(sitting), Robert Beriault

I left St. John's Rehab shortly after that and returned home full time. I used the sidewalk that went around our block and walked it twice a day. After two months of walking, I went out and tested myself by walking five kilometers with rests along the way and successfully completed it. So, with one month to go before the walkathon, I knew I could make the distance. Further, my fund-raising efforts were going extremely well. I had set a goal of $20,000, and when I completed the walk I had raised over $23,000.

With that first-year success under my belt, I decided I would commit to the "Steel Legs Walk" and the JDRF for five years and attempt to raise $100,000. My health, my kidney and my legs were doing well, so I saw no reason not to make this my long-term goal.

However, in my third year, I unexpectedly suffered heart problems during the walk. I managed to complete the walk but was extremely tired throughout. We went to the hospital and after an angiogram, it was discovered I had a blockage in my right heart artery. An angioplasty was advised and it corrected the situation. As a result of this successful heart surgery, I completed five successful "Steel Legs Walks" and my generous donors contributed a total of $106,810.00.

STEEL LEGS WALK
Juvenile Diabetes Research Foundation – J.D.R.F.

Year #	Goal	Actual	Cumulative
1	$20,000	$23,000	$23,000
2	$20,000	$18,750	$41,750
3	$20,000	$20,300	$62,050
4	$20,000	$20,565	$82,615
5	$20,000	$24,195	$106,810
TOTAL			$106,810

It was exactly one week after my fifth and last "Steel Legs Walk" that I was called to the University Health Network's Toronto General Hospital for a pancreas transplant. I had waited almost two and a half years to get this opportunity to end fifty-five years of Type 1 diabetes.

Steel Legs Walk – Steve Beriault

Tale # 9
ON THE RIVERS

One summer, I attempted to kayak the old fur-trading river route through western Canada known as the Voyageur Route.

My first memory of canoeing and kayaking on the water was at diabetic camp. I loved the way the craft would cut and skim through the water, and I loved the feel of the paddle stroke as my arms, shoulders and body unleashed power down the paddle's length and became one with it.

It is a simple process to learn how to paddle a canoe or kayak: you have to enjoy the physical rhythmic cadence of the stroke. It matches the cadence of the heart that beats in your chest and drives you inexorably forward. Once you discover that feeling, then turning, guiding, backwater, figure eights and other maneuvers are simple to add on from that basic process.

However, as a Type 1 diabetic with too much energy to expend, I found myself falling into diabetic insulin reaction in the middle of the lake on different occasions.

One time, although I was in the canoe by myself, I did have other paddlers around me as we raced across the lake. In this instance, I had a good lead on the flotilla. But I lost my strength. Although my spirit was high and excitement ran in my veins, I couldn't drive the paddle. It became as heavy as stone. As the pack caught up, my paddle was dangling in the water from one hand and I didn't know where I was.

One of the counselors said, "Hey, why are you slacking off?"

I didn't respond because I couldn't make out what he was saying. They soon figured out what was wrong and got me back to shore to take some "Coke syrup" (this was the thick sugar/cola concentrate used to make the beverage Coca Cola) to elevate my blood sugar.

During my high school days, I joined a local canoe club and had the opportunity to race in war canoes and single, double and four-man racing kayaks as well as single, double and four-man racing canoes. The experiences were wonderful and sometimes very "upsetting," especially if you were out on a lake or river with a high wind or a large thunder and lightning storm coming towards you. The racing craft were built with shallow hulls and low sleek sides to reduce the drag in the water. That also meant that with inexperienced paddlers, they would tip easily in waves or rough weather. Fortunately, this is not so much the case with sport kayaks and canoes with deeper hulls and not extremely sleek low sides.

I raced in "open canoe" ten-mile events with my pal Pat (who became a doctor) on the mighty Ottawa River. Later, we raced, led by our determined and strong captain Duane (who became a teacher), on the Saugeen River (Walkerton to Paisley) for thirty-five miles in their annual community distance race. Our team of six paddlers (two per canoe) finished 1-2-3 in the "open canoe" segment of the race.

In this race, my friend Dennis and I were paired together (I was Dennis and Jane's best man). There were so many racers in canoes, kayaks and other craft at the starting line that we got caught in a traffic jam of boats when the gun went off. We finally broke free from the pack about a mile downriver but saw that quite a few of our competitors had gotten a good lead over us. We worked hard to catch up but we would never last thirty-five miles at that pace. We needed a break. As we came around the bend of the river and approached the dam, our first portage, we decided we would not portage around the dam to make up for lost time. It was a big risk!

We aimed our canoe directly at the one open sluice where water was pouring over the dam. We drove our paddles as hard as we could and sliced through the open segment of the dam. We flew in the air with the force of the water pushing us along and landed (luckily) flat on our canoe bottom. We managed to keep our balance and continued stroking past our competition, now caught pulling and carrying their canoes and kayaks around the dam through the forest. We figured we gained at least twenty minutes with that gutsy and lucky move.

The kayak that I bought for my trip along the old Voyageur Route through Western Canada was found at a secondhand sale in Port Coquitlam in British Columbia. I had attended school at Simon Fraser University on Burnaby Mountain and made a decision to take the summer off. I planned a kayak trip from Banff to Winnipeg using the old fur-trader route of the voyageurs and coureurs de bois.

Beginning on the Bow River just below Bow Falls in Banff, I would travel on it to the Old Man River (these two rivers merge to become the South Saskatchewan River), then head northeast on the South Saskatchewan to Lake Diefenbaker, the Qu'Appelle dam and river and then on to the Assiniboine River to Winnipeg. This is where the old North West and Hudson Bay fur-trading posts were located. I was taking a little adventure through Canadian history.

I trained in the Burrard Inlet in Vancouver to get used to my kayak and to get my body in shape for the 1,700 kilometer adventure I was to undertake. All my gear fit under the front and back gunnels of the kayak, and once in there they would not get soaked by the elements. Under the gunnels I stored my sleeping bag, tent, spare clothes, army rain poncho (cut so it didn't drag in the water while paddling), hunting knife, small hatchet, insulin supplies stored in a waterproof container and other camping essentials.

My food supplies were a huge waterproof sack of trail mix and several packets of freeze-dried meals, which you added water to and heated over the fire. I used water purification pills to drink the river water from my canteen. Finally, I had a small extendable fishing rod to attempt some fishing along the way. Of course, I carried my Billy Bee honey.

The last thing to include when you were ready to enter the boat was the elastic rubberized skirt, which was pulled on like a pair of pants up to your waist. Then you sat down on your kayak seat and pulled the elastic skirt around the seat opening to seal it from water dripping from your paddle and rain. It was also necessary for the "Eskimo roll" if your kayak should tip and roll in the open water due to high winds or white water rapids.

My insulin regime was one 35-unit shot of long-acting (ultralente beef/pork) per day. I carried short-acting insulin with me on days I might not be paddling to compensate for potential higher blood sugar levels. It was a simple credo: the more you worked, the less need for insulin; the more you sat around, the more insulin you needed to keep your blood sugar under control. (Blood sugar monitoring devices were still not available at that time).

I drove my beat-up old Ford Fairlane (1965) with my kayak on it to Banff, where my brother Mike met me. Mike would take my car to Calgary and store it for me until I returned for it (which would be at his marriage to Karen in Calgary, in August). We placed the kayak in the crashing whitewater just below Bow Falls. It was hard to speak and hear each other clearly but I managed to yell to him I should be in Calgary in three to four days. He said, "See you there." With that I was off on my adventure down the Bow River. The water was fast and rushed me downriver quickly. It was also very cold, as the Bows' headwaters are glacier fed (as are those of the Old Man and South Saskatchewan Rivers) in the Rocky Mountains.

The sheer beauty of the mountains and the magnificent scenery was amazing. The mountains reminded me of huge cathedrals: so stately, powerful and serene. These cathedrals were built by God, for no man, even in his wildest imaginings, could imitate or come close to copying these superlative structures or their gargantuan dimensions. I was on a definite Rocky Mountain high! Then I started singing John Denver songs as I went down the river in a total state of joy and exuberance. The river flew by and I saw schools of small fish flee from the dark shadow of my boat on the aquamarine, crystal-clear waters.

As I got further out of the mountains and on to the foothills, the river slowed slightly and wound its way through cattle territory. Here, the embankments became larger where the river cut the soil. As I came around a bend, I saw a huge bull lying down on the edge of the embankment. One of his legs was dangling over the embankment and the other was crooked in front of it, tucked into his body. He seemed completely relaxed and was breathing deeply. As I got closer, he appeared to be sleeping. I was upwind from him, so he didn't catch my scent, and I was letting the current carry me towards it, so I wasn't making any noise.

It was at the moment I was directly across from the bull that I let out a loud "MOOOOO!" He reacted with a sudden leap directly into the air and a ferocious snort. But his leap up resulted in his misjudging where the lip of the embankment was. He landed with a splash, with both front feet down the embankment into the water. His snout went under water as well, and both hind legs were stuck high above him. He lifted his head in this very funny position and snorted water out of his nose as he shook his head aggressively. I was laughing so loudly that I had tears in my eyes as I paddled hard to get out of there.

I had to maneuver past four dams on my way east on the river. The first one was the Ghost Dam, the farthest upstream from Calgary. The Ghost Dam was built in 1911. It was the first dam on the Bow River. The second dam was the Horseshoe Dam and it was downstream from the Ghost, close to the community of Morley. The third dam was the Bearspaw Dam and it was close to Cochrane, Alberta. The fourth and largest dam was called the Bassano Dam and it was very far downstream from Calgary, near the western community of Bassano and near the intersection of the Bow and Old Man/South Saskatchewan Rivers.

Getting around the Ghost Dam was a brand new experience for me. In my training on Burrard Inlet, I had never had the opportunity to scale a dam with kayak and gear. So as I moved from a swift-water river into a long lake of backed-up water, I started to get a little nervous about what exactly I would have to do to get around the obstacle. I brought the kayak right to the center of the dam and climbed out on its lip. Helpfully, there were steel pegs in the concrete where I could secure the boat and scout around to figure out how I was going to maneuver myself and my gear down into the gorge below.

There were a couple of options: (1) I could carry or drag the boat and gear on the high prairie around the dam and gorge and climb down into the gorge where it wasn't as steep downriver, or (2) I could take the direct route right here at the dam and scale down into the gorge immediately and get back on the water

I found a good set of rock outcrops that I could use to lower my kayak and gear by rope into the gorge on the right side of the dam. Tying my rope to the front of the kayak, I lifted it and pointed it straight down till it rested on the first outcrop. As it balanced there, I climbed down beside it. The next outcrop was much further down and I had to lower the kayak by rope and try to target the swinging boat on the next outcrop. After a few attempts, it finally nestled where I wanted it. The final section was another long drop, for which I had some difficulty positioning the boat because the rock outcrop was smaller and rounder in configuration. I must have worked for fifteen minutes getting the kayak positioned and repositioned to sit on that rock. My arms were aching from the effort of holding the rope attached to the weight of the dangling kayak. Toward the end, I thought I would have to climb back up and take the land route around the dam.

But luck was with me; the boat finally clung to the rock outcrop and I quickly climbed down to it. From there I was only a meter from the river bottom and I lowered the boat into the water using my rope. I tied my kayak to a rock on the riverside and climbed back up to get my gear. I loaded my stuff into the boat and climbed in. The gorge was cut out of solid grey-black rock, and I wondered how many thousands of years and trillions of gallons of water had poured down this gorge to shape it into the art forms that I was viewing. The walls were shiny with wear and about thirty feet high. I felt that I was traveling in some sacred place as my paddle strokes echoed along the high silent walls.

As I proceeded down the channel, the water began to move more quickly, and ahead of me I saw the gorge suddenly narrowed, with two vertical stone columns on either side. The river dropped away from sight and I heard the sound of rapids. I moved to the right side, out of the current, and came in close to the vertical column, where I knew the backwater would be. The kayak settled easily along the rock wall and I climbed out. I tied the boat to a stone and started to climb up the rock face because I wanted to scan from above what I was getting into.

I grabbed a handhold on a protruding rock and pulled up to find myself staring right into the face of a beaver. It was so unexpected that I almost lost my grip. The beaver was just as stunned as I was over this surprise meeting and reflexively jumped and turned to escape. But the rock wall was behind it and its head hit the wall. It then turned quickly and jumped over my shoulder and into the river below. I watched its bobbing head swiftly disappear around the rocks and down into the gorge. I continued climbing a little more cautiously and got to the top, where I had a good view of the white water.

The water dropped immediately about four feet,

then continued with rapids for about 150 yards and then returned to its normal character. It looked to me that the best way to get over the small falls was to aim the kayak to the left side of the vertical stone column. The right side had some clearly evident boulders, which I could hit and roll over, while the left side did not. The rapids were not turbulent enough, in my estimation, to cause me any concern.

So I climbed back down, got into the kayak and back paddled along the wall to get some running room at the falls. I turned the boat into the current and drove as hard as I could with my paddle to get speed to get over the falls. The faster I went the more likely I would keep my balance and not upset (like cycling a bicycle) when I landed. Sure enough, things went according to plan and the run through the rapids was fun.

I had to work my way over two more dams before reaching Calgary, which I did successfully. I arrived on the outskirts of Calgary and climbed up the embankment at the first bridge to try to find a phone. Luckily, there was a service station close to the bridge and I called my brother Mike, who came to pick me up. I visited a couple of days with Mike, his fiancée Karen and the soon to be in-laws, the Schellenbergs. It was a great visit and the Schellenberg family drove me out to the east side of the city to restart my trip on the Bow River. It was here that I learned that the western prairies were experiencing a drought that had started in early spring, and the river systems were low from lack of rain and snow in the mountains.

In two days' time, I came to the fourth and largest dam on the Bow River near the community of Bassano. The river flowed into a big lake basin, at the far end of which was the dam. I did not bother to go directly on to the dam because it looked huge; I decided instead to land on the left hand side of the dam. There I would portage across the rolling prairie to find a lowering of the embankment to get myself back into the river.

So I landed, tied my rope to the front of the boat

and started hauling the kayak through the prairie grass. Actually, the smooth fiberglass hull of the boat skimmed easily along the grass-shrouded ground. I traveled about an hour in this way but still found the gorge too high to attempt to launch the kayak. I ate trail mix as I walked along and I drank from my canteen.

I saw an old gray Dodge truck, its front right panel dented, come across the ridge line above me about two hundred yards away. The driver must have spotted me because he immediately changed direction, bouncing the truck over the ridge line and down to the lower area where I was walking. I stood and waited to see what would happen.

The driver drove up right beside me and stopped. He looked at me curiously but didn't say anything. He was an Indian, about twenty years old, ruggedly handsome and deeply tanned, of medium build with a straw cowboy hat on his head. I stood there and waited for him to say something. But after a long silence I guessed he was waiting for me to explain myself, so I broke the silence by saying I was portaging around the dam to get to a lower part of the river to launch my kayak.

He grinned a little and I'm sure he must have thought I was crazy. Then he raised his hand and pointed to the kayak and then used his thumb to indicate to me to put it in the back of the truck. As he raised his thumb to point backwards, I suddenly realized he had a gun rack in the cab with three rifles hanging there. That made me a little nervous but I kept that to myself as I loaded my kayak and gear into the truck. I climbed into the back with my gear and hoped he knew where he was going. With a wave of his hand out the window to me, he took off over the open prairie with me banging and clunking in the back with my kayak and supplies.

We traveled for awhile in an easterly direction on the prairie and I felt good about that, as that was the correct direction I wanted to go on the river. Suddenly he came to a jolting halt, grabbed a rifle from the rifle rack in the cab of the truck, bolted out of his door and aimed the rifle towards the ridge line we were following. Needless to say, a few scary thoughts passed through my mind in that instance.

He waited, looking for something, but I had no clue what it was. I was looking up on the ridge when a large deer appeared in full sight. The young man fired almost immediately and the deer jerked and balanced for moment on the ridge and then toppled over and rolled down the incline. The young man yelled triumphantly across the prairie in a loud voice.

He leaped back into the cab (I think he had completely forgotten I was in the back of the vehicle) and drove over to his kill. He jumped out of the truck and unsheathed a hunting knife and began gutting the deer. He did it quickly and efficiently and then dragged the carcass over to the truck. He had a big smile on his face and seemed very proud of his accomplishment. He waved his hand at me and wanted me to help him load the deer into the back of the truck. So I pushed my kayak and gear as close to the right side of the truck as possible, jumped down and helped him load the carcass.

He laughed with great pleasure when we got the carcass onboard and clapped me on the shoulder to say thank you. He then indicated I should climb in front with him and we drove some miles over the open prairie. Finally we came to a depression in the embankment that allowed me to launch the kayak. As I got the kayak into the water, I turned to say goodbye but he was already walking to his truck. I yelled out, "Thanks," and he simply raised his arm in farewell and got into his truck and left. I smiled to myself as I envisioned the young man getting home to tell his friends and family about the crazy white man he saw pulling a boat across the open prairie!

Within a short time, I reached the intersection of the Bow and Old Man Rivers. The swift South Saskatchewan River was the result of this watery union—the rivers were simply a geographical extension of each other. Both rivers cut deep into the prairie soil and had high embankments from which, if you took the time to climb, you would view long vistas of open rolling prairie as far as you could see. However, not many houses or people were in sight.

I arrived at Medicine Hat and only realized that I was in the city by traveling under the Trans-Canada Highway bridge that leads into the city. It had a small, badly painted, upside-down red sign on it that said "Med. Hat," probably done by some teenager hanging upside over the bridge as a graduation night dare. I paddled about a half mile down from the bridge, tied my boat up on the shore and hid it with tree branches. Then I climbed the high embankment with my gear searching for the Medicine Hat Hostel. I was in heaven in the hostel. I took a long shower and enjoyed lying on a soft bed. I then went to a local restaurant and had a great meal and shot up short acting insulin with my long-acting baseline to compensate for the carbohydrate load. Then I went back to the hostel to sleep.

I awoke early and had a delicious breakfast at the hostel. Then I grabbed my stuff, climbed back down the embankment and got my kayak back on the fast-moving river. The South Saskatchewan takes a northeasterly route from Medicine Hat up to the Qu'Appelle River. The South Saskatchewan winds through one of the deepest canyons on the Canadian prairies. This enormous geographic formation was used to contain Lake Diefenbaker. The lake is actually the reservoir of the huge Gardiner Dam, which stretches almost two miles across, and the lake is about 160 miles long. The Gardiner Dam is one of the largest earth-filled dams in the world.

After ten days of travel up Lake Diefenbaker, I arrived near the Qu'Appelle Dam. I had been lucky on the way and caught fish each day on the lake. Freshly cooked fish is extremely tasty. The Qu'Appelle River originates at the outlet dam on Lake Diefenbaker. A short distance from the Qu'Appelle dam, I came upon three guys fishing in a boat. I noticed they had no fish but they were happy drunks. I asked, "How is the fishing expedition going?"

One young fellow answered, "This ain't no fishing expedition—this is a drinking expedition!"

I started to laugh and they followed suit.

"Hey, where you goin'?" one asked.

I said, "I want to get over the Qu'Appelle dam and continue down the Qu'Appelle River."

They all said, in unison, "We can help you do that."

I soon followed them to an old truck parked on the beach. They helped load my stuff into the truck and drove across back roads because they "didn't want the cops to catch them." After several miles and two wrong turns, we arrived at the edge of the Qu'Appelle River. They wanted me to stay the night and drink with them but I said I had to get going. They wished me luck and said, "Come back and visit with us anytime— you're a good buddy!

The river flows southeast from its origin to the junction with Last Trail Creek. The Qu'Appelle River winds through many lakes on its journey to the Assiniboine River in Manitoba. The river also seemed full of whitefish, which I dined upon several times along with my trail mix.

It was here that I traveled for miles down a peaceful valley setting. The river meandered greatly through the soft prairie soil, causing miles of extended travel. Sometimes I would stop along the way to climb an embankment to look around. It was just open prairie, and occasionally I would see oxbow lakes scattered throughout the area where the Qu'Appelle River once flowed. (An oxbow is a crescent-shaped lake lying alongside a winding river. The lake is created over time as erosion and deposits of soil change the river's course.)

"The Legend of Qu'Appelle Valley" is a poem by E. Pauline Johnson that recounts the legend of a young Indian who, upon returning from a hunting trip, hears a voice. He replies "Who calls?" in Cree, and then in the language of the French settlers—"Qu'appelle?" but receives no answer save his echo. When he does return to the tribal village, he discovers that the young woman he was to marry has died suddenly and, with her dying breath, cried out his name. And thus, the Qu'Appelle Valley received its name. I called out many times on the

Qu'Appelle River and got my echo, and I also heard sounds on the wind that I thought were whispering to me. It was spooky but very interesting, and I would listen as intently as possible to pick up my echo or understand the whispering when the wind sighed.

After several weeks on the river, and after passing many large beach areas where people were enjoying the water in the hot, dry conditions, I came to Fort Qu'Appelle. I noticed the water was low in the lakes as the drought continued. The water marks were much higher than where the actual water line was. I came upon a good area to park my kayak just below a cottage, where an elderly gentleman was sitting.

I went up to him, introduced myself, and asked if he would mind if I left my boat there overnight. Tony said, "No bother at all." Then he asked me what I was doing, so I sat with him a while and told him about my trip. I then said I was going into Fort Qu'Appelle to stay at a motel, sleep on clean sheets and have a very long shower. He laughed at that and then said, "I'll drive you into town and I'll come and have breakfast with you tomorrow morning before you leave."

I said, "Great! But don't come before 10 a.m. because I'm sleeping in."

He left me at the motel, which was located right beside a restaurant. I brought my gear up to the room, which had a king-sized bed, and I jumped for joy on top of it and almost immediately fell asleep. Several hours later, I awoke, had a long relaxing shower, put on my clean jeans and fresh T-shirt and went out to eat. I took a shot of regular insulin to compensate for indulging myself. I was very pleased with my lack of insulin reactions (hypoglycemia) over the length of the trip until then. I had eaten well with the fish I caught and my freeze-dried meals. But I believe that munching every so often during the day on the trail mix that I carried with me was helping to keep my sugars out of hypoglycemic range.

I was up at nine, showered, packed all my washed

clothes and, sure enough, heard the phone ring at precisely 10 a.m. Tony met me downstairs and we walked across to the restaurant for breakfast. He was a retired farmer who had lost his wife years before. His two sons were working in British Columbia and he did not see them often. His health, humor and appetite were very good and he kept asking me why I didn't eat much since I was getting a freebie, and then he laughed.

Unknown to me, he had asked the waitress to cook up a mess of peameal bacon, regular bacon and hash browns and wrap it all in silver foil in a waterproof container. I was handed the feast as we were leaving the restaurant, and it was all paid for by Tony. I thanked him and waved goodbye on the river. He yelled, "Good luck, young fella!"

It was here along the Qu'Appelle River that I had two memorable bird experiences. As I came around a large meander in the river, I spotted a duck hen with her goslings swimming ahead of me. They hadn't seen my kayak yet as they went about their business. I came closer without making a sound. The goslings were wonderful to watch as their little bottoms moved furiously in time to their paddling feet. They were in triangular formation behind their mother.

Suddenly, the mother reacted as she saw me and quacked loudly and the whole group picked up the pace. As I watched, I could swear the goslings were starting to disappear as the triangle became smaller. Sure enough, some of the little ones were diving under water and resurfacing on the shore line. With three goslings still left, the mother began to play lame in the water to attract my attention while the three little ones dove underwater.

The mother continued the deception for awhile, leading me upstream, and then broke into flight leaving me behind. However, I waited till she was out of sight and circled and went back up river, as close to the embankment as I could get, and waited. Suddenly the mother came in low over the embankment and settled into the water.

Shortly afterwards, the goslings began to appear around her one by one. I thought how courageous an act this was and how well executed by the little ones and their mother.

A few days later, I encountered another large swath of meandering river and at the last turn, I came upon a very high steep embankment. All was quiet and I stopped for a minute to rest and slowly floated towards the embankment. Suddenly, the whole face of the embankment exploded with movement.

I thought that the embankment was caving in on the river. Loud bird squawks, twittering and hundreds of wings whooshing in the air surrounded me. I was completely engulfed in flying birds. Actually, the whole embankment was a nesting place for hordes of birds. As my initial scare wore off, I saw hundreds of tiny holes drilled into the embankment. Also, I found bird excrement over the front and back of my kayak and on my hat as well. I felt I was being warned, "Don't bother the Saskatchewan wildlife."

The water and the quiet, interrupted only by my paddle strokes; the wind blowing through the trees; bird calls and sometimes cows "mooing" somewhere above me on the river's edge: all these made this river very magical and serene. The dams along the Qu'Appelle numbered seven, and sometimes the river was very shallow because of the continuing drought in western Canada. It would vary in width from ten feet to a hundred feet across or turn into a lake. My kayak scraped bottom in some places because of the low water levels.

I came upon one of several small lakes as I continued eastward to the Assiniboine River. Here, as I glided along the shore line, I spotted a beaver floating in the water gnawing on a small branch. Its back was to me and I was upwind from it. I continued as silently as I could and it seemed totally unaware of my presence.

I was about three feet to its left as I coasted by and I saw its nostrils flare, its eyes open wide and it quickly dived with a funny "gluck" sound and no tail warning for its comrades. When beavers are aware of anything on the river that shouldn't be there, they usually dive, but they whack their big flat tails on the water as a warning sound to their comrades. This poor beggar was so caught by surprise that he couldn't do anything except get under water. I wondered if the "gluck" sound was it swallowing water when it dived in surprise!

So I continued down the river, chuckling to myself about catching the beaver off guard and the funny sound it had made. It was no more than a few minutes later, as I was focusing on making a turn around a point in the lake, when a loud bang (I thought it was a gun) occurred just to the back and left of me. I almost tipped over with the unexpected sound, but the water wasn't deep and I dug my paddle into the bottom of the lake to keep me upright.

Once I caught my breath, I quickly looked back to see what had happened. I saw nothing immediately, so I waited. Then I saw the small head of a beaver appear about twenty yards up the lakeshore from me. It pulled up on the shore and looked back at me and started to make a fast clicking sound with its teeth, which I interpreted as it laughing at me. Payback is fun even for animals.

Up to this point on the trip, I had not experienced any low blood sugar episodes, which surprised me. Maybe it was the slower pace of travel and resting when I wanted, as the river current carried me persistently eastward towards my destination. I faced no direct headwinds in the low river bottoms and therefore did not have to fight against that disadvantage.

However, I did have one hypoglycemic episode, on a small lake approximately one mile long in the Qu'Appelle river system. I got out to the middle of the lake when I became disoriented and thought I was moving in a westerly direction instead of easterly. So I turned the kayak around and proceed in the opposite direction. After a short time, I noticed a previous landmark that indicated I was heading back west. So I turned the kayak around and headed east again. I must have gone in circles like this for awhile when I became so weary that my shoulders could not hold up the paddle.

At first, I was trying to explain to myself why I couldn't paddle anymore. I thought the paddle was too short. Then I said it was too long. Then I said one of the paddles was missing. Then I was discussing in my head why my muscles wouldn't work. I thought it could be a nerve issue, strained muscles, lactic acid, injury, strain, ligament damage and finally I fell upon the word "glucose." No glucose, no energy. No energy, no paddling. "Hmm," I thought, "that sounds like a good reason." So once I got agreement in my mind on the problem, I had to find the glucose. I tried to remember where I'd put my glucose, but I was coming up blank. I kept seeing a yellow color in my mind but didn't understand what it meant. Suddenly, an image came to mind and I saw my yellow Billy Bee honey container under my seat in the kayak. With trembling hands I pulled off my waterproof seat cover and grabbed my Billy Bee. I got myself out of my predicament all right and made camp right there on the beach of the small lake with no name.

With the current on the rivers moving me at a continual pace and with my paddling usually from sunup to sundown, I estimated I was doing about thirty to forty kilometers a day. I paddled into another lake on the Qu'Appelle and followed its shoreline. As I came near a narrowing where the river started its course again, I saw a wood sign stuck sideways into the ground with the name Bird's Point on it. If that was correct, I was only a short distance from the Assiniboine River. It was near here that Mother Nature suddenly ended my river travels.

I moved on by two days past Bird's Point and I noticed that the sky was starting to darken in the late afternoon. From the signs in the sky, I would say the drought ridden prairies were going to get some rain this evening. I camped early because I found a great place to camp. Not only did I have a large overhanging tree to tie my boat to, but up on the top of the high embankment I had shrubs and small trees growing as well, which would help protect my tent from the wind and rain, which I expected. In fact, the wind was starting to pick up and I could see dark clouds on the horizon as I entered my tent.

The wind blew for a long time as my tent flaps rippled with the force. It started to thunder and lightning with great frequency and I could see the bright flashes through my tent wall. Finally, the rain poured out of the sky around 3:30 a.m. as though someone had opened a faucet. The rain hit with such force that the tent—even with the cover from the bushes and trees—began to wobble with the impact. I found myself supporting the tent pole so it wouldn't topple over. The impact and volume of rain quickly eroded the rain-proofing material I had sprayed on the tent. Drops of water began falling into the tent and there was nothing I could do about it.

So I waited inside the tent, holding the tent pole steady, as the storm blew around me. The great deluge of water from the sky subsided in about half an hour, but the storm continued and it rained steadily after that. I considered that the prairie farmers would be thankful for this rain after several months of parched land.

I glanced at my watch and saw that it was 5 a.m. and I thought it would soon be dawn. The rain had tapered off considerably and the sun broke in the east as patches of blue sky let the light through. I saw the light through my tent wall and decided to go outside. I was reaching for my tent-door zipper when I felt myself sliding down. The tent collapsed around me and I was falling.

I remember striking something along the way on my left side but I didn't think much of it at the time. I landed in the river and felt the water surrounding my legs. I was still caught in the unopened tent and I couldn't find the doorway. I kept my knife with me on my belt so I pulled it out and slashed the nylon fabric that engulfed me. I hauled myself out of the tent and then pulled it on to shore with me, as all my supplies were in it.

The rain had stopped and nothing but silence hung over the river. It now seemed as if nothing had happened at all. The quiet was like a classroom of kids who had performed some willful escapade while the teacher was away, but when the teacher asks what happened, the response is silence. I looked around to see that about twenty yards of embankment had given way and slid into the river. Trees, shrubs and gumbo were all stretched out into the water.

"My kayak!" I yelled. Where was it? After some rummaging around in the muck I found it. The tree that I had tied my boat to had fallen. The kayak had been crushed into a V-shape by the force of the fall and then engulfed in thick gumbo from the slide. My heart sank. I was close to the Assiniboine and it was maybe 250 more kilometers to Winnipeg. What a way to end my trip! I thought I had been unfairly treated by Mother Nature and was angry. I yelled out, "You did this!" And in the quite silence I heard the mocking echo: "You did this! You did this! You did this!" Mother Nature neither cared nor was interested in what I thought was fair or unfair. She had bigger fish to fry.

So I sat in the mud for awhile in despair until I noticed the ache in my side. I had a bad bruise just below my arm on the left side of my chest. What the heck, I thought. I figured it was just a bruise and didn't think anymore of it. I gathered my remaining stuff and struggled back up the embankment. The gumbo was difficult to climb in and I half slid, half climbed to the top. When I got to the top, I took a deep breath and almost passed out from the sharp pain in my chest. I decided my bruised side was probably cracked or broken ribs.

In any case, I was in the middle of nowhere and I knew there were villages and roads to the south of me. So I started walking with my backpack across a grassy prairie field. It was about two miles long and then it turned into a ploughed field with water puddles standing out clearly all over it. I looked in every direction to find a way not to fight my way across this field of gumbo soil. No such luck: I plodded along through the rich, thick clay mud. It took a lot of work and I tried to keep my breathing under control because, if I drew in a large breath, a deep pain would shoot through my chest. I walked a very long distance until, on the ridge ahead, I saw a truck pass by. It was a road.

Exhausted, I sat on the edge of a gravel road and rested. No vehicles passed by while I waited. I later used my backpack as a pillow and lay on my right side and fell asleep. When I awoke, I grabbed some rocks from the road and attempted to clean the muck off my shoes. I then noticed my T-shirt had mud smeared on it, as did my shorts. I took my T-shirt off and pulled on a fresh T-shirt from my pack. I then scrubbed my shorts with prairie grass to get some of the mud stains off. However the mud stains were still on my arms and clumps were stuck in my hair. It was while I was trying to get the mud out of my hair that an old Ford truck came down the road. I very hesitantly put out my thumb to see if I might get a drive.

The driver, an older man with a baseball cap, slowed and stared and lowered his sunglasses in surprise as he went by me. He looked back twice at me through his back window and then finally stopped about a hundred feet up the road. I grabbed my stuff and ran to the truck. When I got up to the open window of the truck, I waited for him to say something. He took a good, long look at me and said, "Well, good Lord, are you ever a mess!" And then he said, "What are you doing way out here on the prairie, fella?" I started to explain myself but as soon as I got to the kayak, he said, "You can tell me the rest on the road, so get in." He told me he was heading to Portage la Prairie and I said that was great. As he drove, I told him my story along the rivers.

Gary dropped me off at a motel in Portage la Prairie and wished me luck. I stayed overnight in Portage, took another long shower, got my clothes cleaned and got my gear in order. I got back on the road with my sore side and wanted to hitchhike to Winnipeg and go to the hospital there, to see if my self-diagnosis was correct. I was picked up quickly by a medical salesman who drove me directly to the hospital he was going to, St. Boniface Hospital in

Winnipeg. He left me at the Emergency entrance and wished me better luck in my travels.

After a long wait in Emergency, I had x-rays taken that indicated I had two cracked ribs on my left side. I was told to relax and take the prescribed painkillers. The doctor said things would start feeling good again in maybe three weeks. I spent a short time in Winnipeg, staying at the Youth Hostel and occasionally a bed and breakfast. I took bus tours of the city and saw the statue of Louis Riel (the founder of the province of Manitoba) beside the Red River. I viewed the Winnipeg Zoo, St. Boniface Cathedral where Louis Riel's remains are buried, and some local museums. Mostly, I rested and slept in and took it easy, as the doctor had ordered. Finally, I couldn't hang around to heal anymore and I went back to the highway to hitchhike home.

I waited about an hour on the Trans-Canada to hitch a ride. The first ride I got was in a big black station wagon driven by a guy, Bill, who was in his forties and wearing sunglasses. He asked me where I was going and I said, "East to Ontario."

He said, "That's where I'm going as well." So I threw my gear into his back seat and settled in. However, I soon learned that he was going to Renfrew, Ontario, just thirty miles past Pembroke, where my home was. Good luck was with me once again!

Tale # 10
PANCREAS TRANSPLANT

The following story is about my failed attempt to free myself from fifty-five years of Type 1 diabetes through a whole pancreas transplant. The pancreas is the organ that produces insulin, via beta cells, whenever your body needs it. A new pancreas would mean I'd never have to inject insulin again. The stress on me and my family was extensive but we all committed to the battle, not realizing how long the fight would take or what the final result would be.

The story starts at 3:45 a.m., Sunday, Father's Day, June 15, as the "beeper" I had been carrying around for the better part of two years (without a sound from it) began to beep. At first, I didn't recognize what the noise was and wrote it off as one of my son's electronic gadgets. It stopped after a couple of minutes and I was dozing off when the phone started to ring. Maria, jumping out of bed, picked up the phone in the office and spoke to whoever it was. She was suddenly at my bedside saying, "Steve, wake up. It's for you."

"Who could be calling at this time?" was my immediate thought.

I soon found out that it was the Transplant Unit at the Toronto General Hospital. I was informed that there was an opportunity for me to get a pancreas transplant but I was not the primary recipient. (That means I was the number two behind the selected patient for the transplant.)

They wanted me to acknowledge to them that I understood that I was number two. I did and I said I was ready to go as soon as they needed me. Then they wanted to know if I had a cold, fever or any sickness. I responded that I did not. They wanted me at the hospital within two hours. After a quick shower and an hour-long drive from Newmarket to Toronto, Maria and I arrived at 5:45 a.m.

On the way there, I was excited and scared at the same time. The operation was six hours in duration and was more complex than my kidney transplant five years earlier. I bounced back and forth from a serious mood to almost giddiness in minutes as we drove. Maria laughed and said, "Don't worry; the stars were aligned in our favor."

I said, "What the hell are you talking about?"

So she informed me that the transplant was to take place on Father's Day, one week after my final successful Steel Legs Walk, a day before her birthday and just two weeks before the York Region School Board, whom she worked for as a social worker, would be off for the summer. She'd come after work to visit me for those first two weeks, but after that she'd be able to spend more time at the hospital without even missing work. Then she said, "This transplant you've waited fifty-five years for is going to happen at last. Wow!"

That sure was positive! However, little did either of us realize what was really going to happen over the next three months. It turned out to be a battle of will power and endurance.

Upon arrival at the transplant wing, we were ushered into a small room with a bed, a chair and curtains pulled around the area to provide some privacy. Although the curtains provided visual privacy, they didn't block out the sounds of voices speaking in the next room. Once we got settled, there wasn't much else to do but sit and wait—and listen. We soon learned that the "primary" was in the next room. He was talking to his girlfriend about being a pancreas transplant recipient.

He did not sound confident or secure in his

commitment to go ahead. Then he and his girlfriend went for a coffee and, as they passed by our room, the curtains parted and we saw this large, long-haired, well-built fellow who looked to be in his mid to late twenties. I thought, "No wonder he's the primary. He's young, looks as healthy as a horse, and is robust and muscular." I figured he was going to get the pancreas transplant while I sat on my duff in the waiting room expecting to be rejected.

Fate had different plans for me. The couple was away for almost forty-five minutes. Nurses came in twice to ask if we knew where the other patient was and we responded that he had gone for coffee. After waiting for almost an hour, the nurses came bustling into our area wanting to take blood from me. While they took my blood, I ventured a question: Where had the other patient gone? I was told that, after some soul searching, the "primary" had decided he didn't want to go ahead with the transplant. So he informed the transplant doctor and left the hospital.

The nurse said, "You are now the primary. However, we have another patient coming as the 'second' in approximately thirty minutes. If, for any reason, your blood type or gene make-up conflicts with that of the donor, we might decide on the 'second' for transplant."

The "second" arrived right on time and was an enthusiastic potential recipient. I got worried again. Our blood tests arrived and the nurses went first to the "second's" room. I thought that was it: he had the better genes and blood match for the transplant.

Minutes later, the "second" left his room and we saw him go by with his wife. We didn't know what to think. Was this really going to happen to a fifty-seven-year-old, balding, kidney-transplanted and double amputated diabetic who had waited for a cure for his diabetes for most of his waking life? The answer was "yes," and the nurses indicated surgery would be around ten o'clock. It seemed the donor's pancreas was an excellent match but still in transit, held up by a storm system in Northern Ontario. (I later learned, after surgery, that a twenty-six-year-old healthy male who had died unexpectedly was my donor.)

Intravenous lines were run, and at approximately ten o'clock, I was wheeled into the surgical theater. I had little time to question or review what was happening, as many nurses and doctors were moving about, getting ready for surgery. They were trapped in their procedures and their own specific thinking processes. Suddenly, the kindly face of an older woman peered into mine and asked, "How are you, honey?"

As I started to reply I blanked out, and awoke approximately six hours later in the step-down unit after my pancreas transplant surgery.

The first thing I mumbled to the nurse was, "What is my blood sugar measurement?" She answered that it was 5.2. (Normal blood sugar measures run about 4 to 6.) The second question was, "Did the surgery go as expected?"

The answer was yes.

I fell back to sleep, happy in the knowledge that the surgery had gone well and my new pancreas was keeping my blood sugar under control. I faded in and out of sleep for most of the day with narcotics reducing the pain. My incision ran in a straight line from my sternum to below my belly button and any movement hurt, even though I had painkillers in my system.

Maria and the boys came to see me later and that made me feel good. Nick informed me a couple of weeks later that all I did was mumble and he didn't understand a word I said. I didn't realize this at the time, but both Nick and Dan pointed out to me that I was covered in plastic tubing carrying saline, medications, blood and whatever else they were shooting into me. I had IV tubes in the arteries of my wrists; in the artery in the back of my neck, which were fed down into my heart; and ordinary IVs in my arm veins. All of these formed a sort of plastic tent over me. It must have been quite a sight but I had no realization of it being there.

I was in the step-down unit for a short time as my vitals were strong, and I was moved to a post-op recovery room. I lost some of my tubes as well, which was cause for some happiness, but I was heavily medicated and still not fully mindful of the world around me. Besides the narcotics for pain, I was taking drugs to prevent rejection of my new pancreas, antibiotics and others, which I couldn't remember. From this interplay of drugs, I became delusional. I suddenly left the reality of being in a hospital room and escaped into a dream world fashioned from visions in my mind. I left the world of normal thought and experience on two different occasions during my three-month stay at hospital.

After my first surgery, the first hallucinatory event lasted seven days, and after my second surgery, the second event lasted eight days. To say I was completely gone during these time periods would be an accurate description. I had no sense of time or place. I occasionally recognized Maria but there was no mental or emotional attachment to her. She was one of the many faces that I saw in the visions in my mind.

In both hallucinatory periods, I dreamed with a "gothic" theme. It was always dark in my dreams; bad things were happening. There was sadness and pain. I had the sense of being overwhelmed but never understanding what was causing this inescapable sensation. I recall shouting out "Show yourself" many times because I wanted to see the hidden enemy causing my fear.

My delusional dreams were in color and full of sensation. I felt the cold, the wind, the rain and the snow in each setting my dream took me to. For me, the make-believe world I was in was real in every sense.

So what delusions did I experience?

My Maria died in a car accident as she raced to the hospital to save me. I held her crushed, bloody body in my arms.

My sons became criminals, robbing and stealing from our neighbors. I kept trying to make things right after their indiscretions—getting them out of jail, paying back my neighbors for their losses—but it continued and continued and I kept paying for their misdeeds. It was endless!

Our house was taken from us through bank fraud and everything Maria and I had worked for was gone.

I was caught in an underground cavern. Huge insects were stalking me and I kept screaming to the people around me (I expect these were nurses but I didn't recognize them) that I needed a weapon to protect myself. No one responded to my cries for help. Finally, desperate to get attention from the silent figures, I threatened to punch somebody if they got close enough. Sure enough, someone bent over me and from far away I heard a male voice saying, "Take it easy." I swung and completely missed, and both my hands were held above my head. (I was later told by Maria, when I became lucid, that the nurses had become frightened by my ranting and raving. They had asked for a security officer to stay in my room, but I had taken a swing at one of the officers. I was then considered a "Code White" and strapped down into my bed, ranting and raving, for sometime.)

And there were even more dreams:

My father and mother died in a car accident and were buried together in the family plot.

My father came back, for some reason, and proceeded to drink and smoke himself to sickness. He died in hospital from cirrhosis of the liver and cancer of the lungs.

My two sons were in a knife fight with some gang and both were stabbed to death.

Overjoyed and thankful, I discovered that my amputated legs were given back to me as a gift from God. Soon I was playing football at my old high school. My new legs were so strong and fast that I stacked up a number of touchdowns against our opposition. I felt young, strong and free. Then something happened, and the football field was shadowed by a huge, dark angel hovering above the field. I was informed by the dark angel from heaven that I had transgressed God's law (although how I transgressed was

213

not outlined to me) and he took my legs away again. I was summarily dumped into a wheelbarrow and taken off the sporting field.

I think you get the general drift of my hallucinations—not very happy. They were very different from my attitude on life and the general happiness I was experiencing in my everyday life. Despite the physical and health challenges I face, I don't look upon the world in this dark way. I have frequently remarked to friends and family that I am the luckiest man in the world. I have experienced some great personal adventures, always made good friends in my travels, have been educated and had a good job, and my family loves me and I them. I couldn't ask for much more in life, despite my weird, dark hallucinations.

In the short time I was lucid after surgery, I kept returning to the thought that my donor was a young man. That caused me some concern after the fact in justifying my selection as the recipient. The young man who died was the same age as my oldest son, Dan, and it struck me how devastating that must be for the donor's family (as it would have been for our family). Further, I got this sense that I didn't deserve the honor of receiving a great gift from such a young man.

It seemed to me that a young man's pancreas should be given to a younger recipient with more opportunities in his life than a fifty-seven-year-old with no legs. It bothered me that I could not come to a resolution about these thoughts and my unworthiness as a recipient of this gift. I finally spoke to a pastor about my concerns and proceeded to become very emotional to the point of weeping. I kept imagining it could have been my own son who died for this purpose.

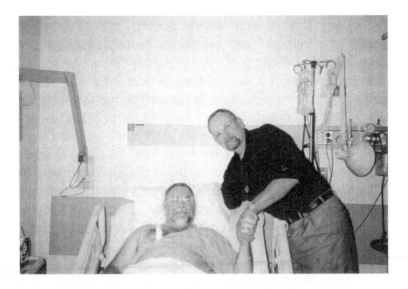

Steve after pancreas surgery with friend *Dr*. Don DuVall

I was an emotional mess, but the pastor kept me on track and we worked through each of the issues. The pastor's final comment to me, as he was leaving, was that our conversation (which lasted almost three hours) was most fulfilling and rewarding for him. I looked questioningly at him. He said that these discussions post-surgery with most other patients usually revolved around issues relating directly to the patient. He mentioned such things as fear, pain, being overwhelmed, ability to cope with limitations and loss of purpose.

He said to me that our discussion had little to do with me; it was about grieving for a family and their lost son. This was related to my own family and the love I have for my sons and the fear of losing them. He said that I did not talk about my diabetes, lost legs, kidney transplant and pancreas transplant or anything that centered on my pain or discomfort. Rather, my focus was other people, as if what had happened to me was not important and not worthy of discussion. He told me I was a very thoughtful and strong individual. "I will remember you when I preach my next sermon," he said, then he shook my hand and left.

My three-month stay in hospital was mainly the result of a cycle of bad infections (notwithstanding my drug-induced delusions of approximately fifteen days). My first major infection was a blood system infection, which caused a bad case of sepsis. It resulted in me throwing up anything I ate; diarrhea; spots forming on my skin, on my hands and arms (some are still there as I write); fever; shaking; and just being very sick. The excellent doctors identified the bacteria causing the problem and treated it effectively. For a few days, I became better and my transplanted pancreas was still working well, with blood sugars in the 5 to 7 range, no matter when or what I ate or if I didn't eat at all.

Then I swung into another major sickness with another bacterial infection in my bloodstream. It took a few days but the medical staff again finally identified the culprit and set the appropriate antibiotic to get rid of it. This occurred several times over the three-month period. My pancreas was not being rejected by my body as it was working perfectly, but something was making my body react as if it were in an infectious state.

It was thought that there must have been a microscopic pinhole in the donor's pancreas tissue that was allowing his bacteria to escape into my system. The hope was that if they could effectively treat the infections, this would give my body the time necessary to heal or plug the small hole.

Further, after several CT scans, the doctors determined that pus was collecting under the skin where my transplanted pancreas was residing. This was causing pressure and pain in my abdomen. I was taken in for surgery on three different occasions to have drainage bags and tubes inserted in my side to drain the affected area. This worked very well and I had these bags attached to me, draining the new transplant, for approximately six weeks.

However, I continued to get sick and had more IV antibiotics given to me. During this time, I was lying continuously in bed and eating nothing solid. I lived on

Jell-O, consommé and broth soup, juices and water, which led me to loose twenty-five pounds (which I needed to lose anyway). My transplanted pancreas continued to work and kept my blood sugar in normal range throughout this whole ordeal. I lost muscle and got weaker; my arms and legs were like jelly.

After almost two months of fighting my problems, the doctors began hinting that things might not work out. They said I had a fifty-fifty chance of success. I said I liked those odds, as long as I was in the fifty percent that succeeded! I said that I was not ready to give up and that I was willing to accept any new treatments or new suggestions to save my very good working pancreas (even though the rest of me was a mess—ha!).

I think they wanted to see how strong my will was in continuing with further interventions. I informed them I was ready and willing. So they attempted different drug combinations and IV mixtures, which reduced the pain and swelling in my abdomen, and soon I had two of my drainage bags removed from my body. Oh joy—that felt so good!

But the hammer was getting ready to fall. One day my drainage bag had blood in it—not much, but it sure attracted a lot of attention from my doctors. They immediately wanted me to take another CT scan and reported to me with very serious faces that the last infection had jeopardized the integrity of the artery close to my pancreas transplant, and therefore it was bleeding a small amount.

However, there was an immediate and urgent need to remove my transplanted pancreas or the artery would continue to lose integrity, and if it burst (an aneurism), I would bleed to death in less than a minute. They would not proceed any further except to perform surgery to remove my still perfectly working pancreas—a pancreas that was not rejected by my body in any way! Instead, all these circumstantial things caused the demise of my dream. The right decision was obvious to me and I went to surgery.

Strangely enough, I did not have emotions or great feelings of loss. I came out of surgery after four hours and asked what my blood sugar was and the nurse said it was 12. I said that sounded like a diabetic blood sugar to me, and I laughed at my own joke. I asked if the surgery had gone well and she replied that it had. And that was it for my eight-week gift of being non-diabetic and having normalized blood sugar. I can only say I fought as hard as I could but the cards were not stacked in my favor.

Also, the final decision to remove the pancreas was not really mine to make; the doctors did it for fear of risking my life. This is what they are well trained to do: recognize dangerous outcomes for their patients and remedy them. After the surgery, one of the doctors asked me if I might re-apply for another transplant attempt. I think he said that because he thought I was devastated by what had happened and felt bad. I said, "No." I figured I was fifty-seven years old and lucky I had gotten the chance and fought my hardest fight. I had nothing else that I could do except be a diabetic till the end of my days and continue to live life to its fullest.

So, after another two weeks in hospital to recuperate, I was moved to St. John's Rehab Unit. I was going to attempt to regain the strength I had lost over so much time in hospital. I had lain on my back, in a sickly state, for almost three months. I stayed a total of three weeks in rehab and progressed rapidly. It almost seemed like my body was dying to do some physical exercise.

It wasn't easy, though. I fell twice at my first attempts at walking. I fell to the floor on my first attempt at climbing stairs, as my legs would not lift my feet up to the first stair. I laughed at my weakness and my clumsiness in trying to walk. The physiotherapists were worrying that I had broken something in falling and wanted me to stay down. It felt good to fall and then struggle to get up. I started to feel alive, pushing myself to get going again.

By the end of my time in rehab, I learned to walk stairs without any problem. I set a record in walking by covering the most distance by a patient in two minutes. My physiotherapist indicated I was traveling at three meters per second. I set the fastest time for any patient on record over the past several years.

The standard set by the physiotherapy association was a ratio between time and distance, with excellent being considered a 0.9. My score was recorded as 1.8 as a double amputee. My effort was twice the standard for excellence. THAT MADE MY DAY! And it took only three weeks to get me moving again! Please don't interpret this score as meaning I am now in good shape, because I am far from it. For example, I was never happier or more relieved when the physiotherapist timing me said "stop" at the end of the two minutes. If I had gone another second, I would have probably fallen on my face! I gave the walk everything that I had.

As I left the rehab unit on my last day, with Maria pushing my wheelchair, she said, "Look, there's Ral sitting in the garden."

I yelled out, "Hey, Ral," and wheeled over to say goodbye. Ral was also a double amputee, but his legs were cut above the knee through his thighs. Furthermore, one leg had healed well but the other had an open sore that would not heal, causing Ral great pain. He was constantly on narcotics. Ral was a smart individual and when he was lucid, we would have interesting conversations.

I said I just wanted to say goodbye and hoped things would get better for him. He said, "Where are you off to?" and I said, "Home." Ral looked away. He had been in and out of hospitals for three years. His legs had originally been cut below the knee (BKA) when he was first treated, but he had to go in for a second amputation on his right leg through his right thigh and finally another cut through his left thigh. His comment was that he was no better than a cheap piece of meat. He said it with a laugh and when he wasn't drugged up, he was witty and had a good attitude about life despite his situation.

I didn't expect his reaction when he turned back to

me. He was weeping. His head and shoulders were drooping as if he were carrying a huge burden. Tears fell into his lap. Maria and I didn't know what to say. We stayed quietly beside him, waiting to see if the emotion would pass. Finally, composing himself, he reached over to shake my hand.

He said, "Steve, you're a good man and have been an inspiration to me and many others with your enthusiasm and energy. People who thought they would never learn to walk with just one leg amputation watched you walk down the hallway with double amputations. You made it look easy and many said, 'If Steve can walk with two legs gone, I can certainly do it with one gone.'"

I started to cry and said, "Good luck, Ral. You're a very brave and courageous person and I hope you find peace with your personal conflict as soon as possible."

We left him sitting in his wheelchair alone in the garden.

I have written a great deal, and if you haven't surmised already, I am writing this for myself, as a reminder of how close I came to fulfilling a dream I have had since a child. My candle has dimmed on my desk. The cold winds of fall are calling for winter, and I must hurry, for I have many other things I must do.

THE HOLLOW MEN

I read T.S. Eliot in high school and my mind was caught by the opening lines of the Hollow Men: "We are the hollow men, We are the stick men." These lines reminded me of the pictures of the diabetic living skeletons I saw in a Medical History book. I viewed that book in the personal library of Dr. Clifford Dobb, my great GP, who cared for me as a boy and teenager. It was in these books that I suddenly realized the courageous but hopeless deaths that diabetics faced without insulin. They looked like prisoners starving in a concentration camp. I never forgot those images, for I realized how easily I could be one of them. These images drive the need for a cure.

DIABETES DIES

We are the hollow men
>We are the stick men

We watch as you live your lives
>on the thin margin

The needles pile up
>and the medications flow

You seek reprieve from this persistent
>scavenger that never relents

Hark! We say to you, many seek the elusive answer
>and struggle to save you
>against darkness; skeptics and
>those who have given up
searching ...   for the knowledge of the cure.

From the past, we call to you
with our voices like thunder

This is how diabetes will die

>Not with a bang
>...................But a whimper.

(Thanks to T.S. Eliot)

Appendix 1
STEVE BERIAULT HbA1C BLOOD MEASURES

(Normal .04 to .064)

Year	HbA1c
2009	0.067
2008	0.055
2008	0.053
2008	0.053
2007	0.073
2007	0.073
2007	0.070
2007	0.072
2007	0.072
2007	0.067
2006	0.066
2006	0.071
2005	0.075
2005	0.069
2005	0.073
2005	0.071
2004	0.066
2004	0.067
2004	0.072
2004	0.073
2004	0.074
2004	0.066
2003	0.062

Appendix 2
THE GLOBAL WAR AGAINST DIABETES

Diabetes Groups of the World

Albania Diabetes Association
Tel. 355/42-33644

Argentina Diabetes Society
Tel. 54-1/813-8419

Diabetes Australia
Tel. 61-6-2835277

Austrian Diabetics Association
Tel. 43-316/385-20608

Bahrain Diabetic Association
Telefax: 937/258-257

Diabetic Association of Bangladesh
Tel. 800 2/86664750

Association Belge du Diabetes (Belgium)
Tel.32-2/374-31-95

 Flemish Diabetes Association
Tel. 32-9/220-05-20

 Bermuda Diabetes Association
Tel. 1 809/292-1595

 Bulgarian Diabetes Association
Tel. 359-2/87-14-97

 Cameroon Diabetes Association
Tel. 237/31 1959 Ext.281

 Canadian Diabetes Association
Tel: 1-416/363-3373

 Association Diabetes Quebec
Tel. 1 514/2593422

 Juvenile Diabetes Research
Foundation (JDRF)
Tel: (905) 944-8700 (Toronto)

 Fondation de la recherche sur le diabète
juvénile .(Montréal) Tel: 514-744-5537

Juvenile Diabetes Foundation of Chile
Tel. 56-2/2288646

Diabetes Society of the Chinese Medical
Association   Tel. 86/5133311

Colombia Diabetes Association
Tel. 57/2880777

Costa Rica Association for Endocrinology
and Diabetes
Tel. 506/332629

Croatian Diabetes Association
Tel. 385/41 23 0991

Cyprus Diabetes Association
Tel.357-2/352568

Czech Diabetes Society
Tel. 422-29 3994

Danish Diabetes Association (Denmark)
Tel. 45-66/12 90 06

Dominican Diabetes Association
Tel. 1809-448-2401 Ext.3458

National Institute of Diabetes (Dominican Republic)
Tel. 809-567-9152

The Egyptian Union of Diabetes
AssociationTel.20-3/4822720

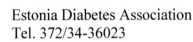

Estonia Diabetes Association
Tel. 372/34-36023

Ethiopian Diabetes Association
Tel. 251-1 /158174

Fiji National Diabetes Foundation
Tel. 679/313444 Ext. 201

Finnish Diabetes Association
Tel. 358-31/2860 111

Association Franquise des Diabetiques
(France)
Tel. 33-1/40 09 24 25

Georgian Diabetes Federation
Tel. 7/8832/51-70-10

German Diabetes Union
Tel. 49-89/8571249

Ghana Diabetes Association
Tel. 233/665401

Hellenic Diabetologic Association (Greece)
Tel. 30- 1/7211845

Grenada Diabetes Association
Tel. 1-809-440-2845

Diabetes Division Society (Hong Kong)
Tel. 852/823-2662

Hungarian Diabetes Association
Tel.36-1-1759922

Diabetic Association of India
Tel. 91-22/273813

Indonesia Diabetes Association
Tel. 62-22/438251

Irish Diabetes Association
Tel. 353-1/363022

Israel Diabetes Association
Tel. 972-3/5270129

Italian Society of Diabetology
Tel. 39-6/44240967

Diabetes Association of Jamaica
Tel. 809-9276744

 Japan Diabetes Society
Tel 81-3/3815-4364

 Kenya Diabetes Association
Tel. 245-2/336725

 Korean Diabetes Association
Tel: 82-2-7949064

 Lebanese Diabetes Association
Tel. 961-1/425-578

 Lithuania Diabetes Association
Tel. 41-81-02

Luxemburg Diabetes Association
Tel. 352/474545

 Malagasy Diabetes Association
(Madagascar)
Tel. 261-2/35058

 Malaysia Diabetes Association
Tel. 60-3/7502385

Maltese Diabetes Association
Tel. 356/454879

Mexico Diabetic Federation
Tel. 52-8/356- 4967

Dutch Diabetes Association (Netherlands)
Tel. 31-33 63 05 66

Dutch Association for Diabetes Research
Tel. 31 20 5487533

Diabetes New Zealand
Tel. 64 3 4348110

Diabetes Association of Nigeria
Tel.234-69/32271 Ext. 10

Norwegian Diabetes Association
Tel. 47-22 65 45 50

Diabetes Association of Pakistan
Tel. 92-21 6616890

Panamanian Diabetes Association
Tel. 507-25-6239

Paraguay Society of Diabetology

Peruvian Diabetes Association (Peru)
Tel. 51-14 730110-244

Philippine Diabetes Association
Tel. 63-2 531 1278

Polish Diabetes Association
Tel. 48-52/21 20 14

Portuguese Diabetes Association
Tel. 351-1 38800041

Puerto Rico Diabetology Society

Russian Diabetes Federation
Tel +7-495-2362442 / +7-495-2362442

Society of Diabetes (Romania)
Tel. 401-6141817

Saudi Diabetes & Endocrine Association
Tel. 966-3/898-695

Diabetic Society of Singapore
Tel. 56/4506-132

Society of Endocrine & Diabetes of
Southern Africa
Tel. 27-21/7837275

South Africa Diabetes Association
Tel. 27-21/4613715

Spanish Diabetic Society

Diabetes Association of Sri Lanka
Tel. 94-1/693375

Sudan Diabetic Association
Tel. 29-11/727-21

Swedish Diabetic Association
Tel. 46-8/629 85 80

Swedish Endocrine Society
Tel. 46-1/6556413

Swiss Diabetes Association
Tel.41-1/383 13 15

Syria Diabetes Association
Tel. 963/440393

Diabetes Association of Thailand
Tel. 66-2/246-4061

The Diabetes Association of Trinidad &
Tobago
Tel. 1-809-622-2382

Tunisian Diabetic Association
Tel. 216-1/570242

Turkish Diabetes Association
Tel. 90-212-230/4900

British Diabetes Association
Tel.44-71/323-1531

American Diabetes Association
1-703-549-1500

Juvenile Diabetes Research Foundation
Phone: 1-800-533-CURE (2873)

Diabetics Association of Uruguay
Tel. 595-21-91-62-14

Venezuela Diabetes Association
Tel. 58-51/535273

Venezuela Endocrine Society
Tel. 58-2/751-37-68

Lightning Source UK Ltd.
Milton Keynes UK
10 July 2010

156795UK00001B/96/P